The PLACE
of the HEART

Cover: The icon of **Our Lady of the Sign** by Sister Cece-
lia, of the Nuns of New Skete, Cambridge, New York, is used
with permission. The icon is based on an icon dating back
to the fourth century which reflects the prophecy of Isaiah:
*"The Lord himself will give you this sign: the virgin shall be
with child, and bear a son, and shall name him Emmanuel."*

Also By Elisabeth Behr-Sigel

The Ministry of Women in the Church
Translated by Fr. Steven Bigham
Oakwood Publications, 1991

Other Offerings from Oakwood

The Art of the Icon: a Theology of Beauty
by Paul Evdokimov
Translated by Fr. Steven Bigham (1989)

The Icon: Image of the Invisible
by Egon Sendler
Translated by Fr. Steven Bigham [1988]

*Dynamic Symmetry Proportional System
Is Found in Some Byzantine & Russian Icons
of the 14th to 16th Century*
by Karyl Knee (1988)

The 'Painter's Manual' of Dionysius of Fourna
ed. & trans. by Paul Hetherington (1990)

*An Iconographer's Patternbook:
The Stroganov Tradition*
by Fr. Christopher Kelley (1992)

Icons & Iconpainting
by Dennis Bell [VHS videotape] (1990)

Icon Collections
by John Barns (1991)

The Place *of the* Heart

An Introduction to Orthodox Spirituality

Elisabeth Behr-Sigel

Translated by
Fr. Steven Bigham

With a contribution
"The Power of the Name;
the Jesus Prayer in Orthodox Spirituality"
by Bishop Kallistos Ware of Diokleia

Ωakwood IPublications

Torrance, California, 1992

Originally published in French under the title:
Le lieu du cœur,
Initiation à la spiritualité de l'Eglise orthodoxe
Les Éditions du Cerf, Paris, 1989

Copyright © 1992 OAKWOOD PUBLICATIONS
3827 Bluff Street, Torrance CA 90505-6359
Telephone and Fax: (310) 378-9245
Orders only: (800) 747-9245

Second Printing 1995

The Power of the Name by Bishop Kallistos
Originally published by
SLG Press, Convent of the Incarnation
Fairacres, Oxford, England, New edition, 1986
© The Sisters of the Love of God 1976
Note: spelling and punctuation have been changed
to reflect North American useage

The *Revised Standard Version* is used for Scriptural quotations

Distributed to the trade by: Source Books

ISBN: 0-879038-04-8

Table of Contents

PREFACE

I am indeed very happy to be able to recommend the two texts published in this work. There is certainly no lack of modern studies on Orthodox spirituality, especially on the prayer of the heart. With one accord, they proclaim the relevance of the spiritual tradition of the Christian East to our times.

The studies of Elisabeth Behr-Sigel and Bishop Kallistos Ware each possess their own originality and are of particular interest to those western Christians, Orthodox or not, who are in search of the heart, that is the quest for a complete and integrated life in Christ, in the breath and light of the Spirit.

Elisabeth Behr-Sigel has captured and described the basic elements of Orthodox spirituality in a penetrating, communicative, and enlightening fashion. I would like to draw special attention to the Scriptural element which is so often passed over in Orthodox presentations. The divine Word, pronounced in the Scriptures, remains forever the foundation of the Orthodox spiritual tradition.

In a time when the Christian faith is being called into question or persecuted by all the materialistic regimes of the planet, the call to martyrdom, one of the basic traits of primitive Christianity, seems to me to be especially up to date and important in our time. This is all the more true because the Christian Churches have not always been able "to resist the temptation of taking up residence in the present age, even to the point of being faint-hearted and servile lackeys of the princes of this world." (Elisabeth Behr-Sigel)

In the same way, the eschatological hope, or more simply the burning and joyful waiting for the return of Christ links our tumultuous period to that of the first Christians. "Earthly life, *here and now*, is already open to eternal Life," to the vision of the Kingdom.

And finally, the theme of the Jesus prayer is attentively studied in the second part of the work by Elisabeth Behr-Sigel as well as in the too short essay of Bishop Kallistos on the power of the Name.

Elisabeth Behr-Sigel presents a picture of the historical development of the hesychastic tradition throughout the centuries, a tradition which became crystallized in the philokalic writings published in the eighteenth and nineteenth centuries in Greece, Moldavia, and Russia. Among these writings, and especially in those of Theophane and Ignatius who were Russian bishops and spiritual masters of the nineteenth century and who were recently canonized (1988), we have a presentation and a modern pedagogy of the "art of prayer."

Bishop Kallistos guides us along a more interior path by recalling several basic elements of prayer: before anything else, silence, that attentive alertness, that listening, that is necessary for God to speak to us and to act. One spiritual master has said that "in prayer, God does everything in everyone." The author suggests a balance between the rule of prayer and the free and spontaneous recitation of the Jesus prayer at all times and in all places.

The invocation of Jesus' name evokes the theology of the Name which goes back through the ecclesial tradition to the biblical sources of God's revelation.

At the end of the spiritual voyage, the invocation of Jesus' name unifies our deep inner being, and our life becomes one with Jesus' life. Our breath becomes one with the divine Breath that sustains the universe. To be carriers of the divine Name is to attain love itself in its source and power. It is to attain God himself, and then "our journey is over. We have arrived at the island that is beyond the world, where we find the Father with the Son and the Holy Spirit." Each one of us becomes "a man for others, living instruments of God's peace and dynamic centers of reconciliation."

Fr. Boris Bobrinskoy

PREAMBLE

This introduction to Orthodox spirituality – it would be more exact to say ". . . to some aspects of Orthodox spirituality" – is part of the theological program offered through the correspondence courses by St Sergius Orthodox Theological Institute in Paris. It is not intended for specialists of Church history or of Christian spirituality. It is rather a modest effort to answer the need of adults who, moved by an intellectual curiosity, are looking for a reasoned presentation of the ecclesial faith and for a deepening of their own spiritual life. I have tried to show how the great, living, and diverse river of Orthodox Christian spirituality came to be constituted. It is a river that has its unique source, for the past and for the present, in the Gospel of Jesus Christ, but it is a current that has also developed in response to historical need, absorbing along the way the richness of various cultures.

This present study is incomplete not only because of my own personal deficiencies but also because of the distribution of tasks among the workers who, 15 years ago, conceived and set up the correspondence program. I felt it necessary to leave to others the presentation on the liturgy as the food and expression of Orthodox spirituality.[1]

---

[1] We have noted the following recent works by French-speaking authors who present the rationale of the liturgy: Constantine Andronikof, *Le Sens de la Liturgie* [The Meaning of the Liturgy], Cerf, 1988; *La divine liturgie de saint Jean Chrysostome* [The Divine Liturgy of St John Chrysostom] and *Les Fêtes et la vie de Jésus-Christ* [The Feasts and the Life of Jesus Christ], in the collection "Catéchèse orthodoxe," Cerf, 1986 and 1985; two new editions of older works, A Monk of the Eastern Church, *L'An de grâce du Seigneur* [The Year of the Lord's Grace] and *L'Offrande liturgique* [The Liturgical Offering], Cerf, 1988.

My own participation in the common work has been aimed at presenting the historical development of the contemplative and mystic current at the heart of Orthodox spirituality. This current is expressed and manifested in the hesychastic movement and in the practice of the Jesus prayer, "the prayer of the heart." But all Orthodox spirituality is not contained in this single aspect, as some have imprudently claimed. It is nonetheless true that the hesychastic movement and the Jesus prayer have deeply marked the tradition. Orthodox spirituality, in its many forms, has never ceased to drink at this great, sometimes invisible, river which today is irrigating new lands in the West. The meditation of Bishop Kallistos Ware is a witness to the creative extension and development of Orthodox spirituality. We thank him most warmly and respectfully for having given us permission to add his meditation as a conclusion to our own study.

Elisabeth Behr-Sigel

INTRODUCTION

The Object of This Study

The word *spirituality* is not found in the traditional vocabulary of Orthodox theology. *Spiritual theology* or *ascetical and mystical theology* are the expressions we normally encounter. The word *spirituality* can suggest a purely psychological analysis of feelings, attitudes, and religious behavior without any reference to the object sought after by the believing person. This point of view is often found in studies of religious psychology. It is not completely devoid of interest, we might add, but this approach opens itself to the superficial confusion of categories. In the realm of human sciences and philosophy, phenomenology[1] has reacted against "psychologism" by noting the impossibility, in our concrete existence, of separating consciousness from the objects to which it turns its attention.

In our study of Orthodox spirituality, we believe it is impossible to separate spirituality from the content of the faith. Vladimir Lossky said that "the eastern tradition has never clearly distinguished between mysticism and theology, between the personal experience of the divine mysteries and the dogma affirmed by the Church."[2] Orthodox spirituality is inseparable from the Good News, the Gospel of Christ

---

[1] The philosophical current that seeks to describe how consciousness registers sense data as it grasps an object. (A method of arriving at absolute essences through the analysis of living experience in disregard of scientific knowledge. *The New Lexicon: Webster's Encyclopedic Dictionary*)

[2] Vladimir Lossky, *Essai sur la théologie mystique de l'Eglise d'Orient* [The Mystical Theology of the Orthodox Church], 1st edition, Paris, 1944, p. 6.

1

announced in and by the Church. This message is offered to all believers who, through the gift of the Holy Spirit, are called upon to assimilate it. Seen in this perspective, Orthodox spirituality is simply the living out of the faith; it is the divine mystery progressively assimilated by each believer. This growth, which takes place within the communion of the "catholic" Church,[3] has an impact on thought, feelings, and concrete attitudes. Again, Lossky writes that "Christian theory has an eminently practical meaning, and this is all the more true because it is mystical."[4]

Spirituality is thus seen as an extension of a theology that, being in line with the spirit and the tradition of the Fathers, aims at an operational understanding of the whole of existence. The highest expression of Orthodox spirituality is *holiness* to which all, clergy and laity, are called, and which is the unification and pacification of the total human person in Christ by the Holy Spirit.

Unity and Diversity

The unity and homogeneity of Orthodox spirituality are assured by Holy Tradition (*paradosis*) which is the transmission of the single message from the birth of the first Christian community under the breath of the Spirit right down to our own time. Tradition is not something inert; it is rather a dynamism, "a movement of Love that diffuses itself,"[5] an "emotion" that propagates itself. The word *emotion* is taken here in its strong etymological sense.

---

[3] The word *catholic* can be translated as *universal*, but from Alexis Khomiakov to Vladimir Lossky, modern Orthodox theologians have emphasized the qualitative aspect of the notion of catholicity in Orthodox ecclesiology. The Church is catholic, *kat'holon*, in that it is oriented toward the fullness of Truth and Grace received in the unanimity of the faith and love. See V. Lossky "Du troisième Attribut de l'Eglise," [Concerning the Third Attribute of the Church], *Dieu Vivant* 10, 1948.

[4] *Ibid.*, p. 7.

[5] A Monk of the Eastern Church, *Notre Père* [Our Father], Beirut, An-Nour, re-edited by Cerf, Paris, 1988, p. 13.

As the breath of the Spirit, Tradition possesses an objective foundation in the Scriptures or, more precisely, in the Word of God pronounced in the Scriptures and explained in the definitions of the ecumenical councils which are sign posts indicating the progress of the spiritual path through history. The divine Word is commented on by the Fathers' teaching as well as in liturgical texts which taken together constitute the expression of the common and correct glorification.[6]

This common ecclesial foundation of Orthodox spirituality does not exclude diversity, however. The one single Light in three Persons is refracted through many individual persons who have communion with Christ by the Holy Spirit. The Church is spread out all over the world and by its long march through the centuries, moving on toward the One who is coming; it has been enriched by its association with various human cultures. In his vision of the heavenly Jerusalem, in Revelations, St John has given us the model for the enrichment of the historical Church: "By its light shall the nations walk; and the kings of the earth shall bring their glory into it, and its gates shall never be shut by day – and there shall be no night there; they shall bring into it the glory and the honor of the nations." (Rev 21:24-26)

Everything that is in man and that aspires by various means to be true, good, beautiful, everything in man that seeks to be delivered and purified, all this belongs already, potentially at least, by the power of the dead and resurrected Christ, to the treasure of the Church.

East and West

In its ascetical and mystical teaching, as well as in its dogmatic theology, the Orthodox Church shows a distinct preference for certain Fathers of the Church who enjoy an

---

[6] We know that the word *orthodoxy* means both "correct belief" and "correct glorification."

unquestioned authority. The liturgical texts call them "the holy hierarchs and ecumenical doctors," among whom we find St John Chrysostom whose theology was simply that of "everyone in the Church," that is the Church's own theology. St Basil the Great is another; his monastic rule has guided millions of men and women on a sure path. St Gregory Nazianzus, also called Gregory the Theologian, is a third of whom Rufinus of Aquileia said that "not to agree with Gregory's faith is an obvious proof of error in the faith."

These spiritual masters are jointly venerated by the East and the West although their influence, like that of the Fathers in general, is less important in the West than in the East In medieval and modern Europe, the influence of the Fathers has been unquestionably eclipsed by other spiritual currents. The result has been an impoverishment that many western Christians are becoming aware of today. Must we therefore conclude that an abyss separates Orthodox spirituality, arbitrarily identified with the Christian East, and western Christian spirituality? A serious analysis, both historical and theological, would not support the notion of such a massive opposition, and it would show that, along with differences that separate and distinguish East from West, there are meetings, exchanges and points of convergence. St Augustine, *the* Father of the western Church who is nonetheless venerated in the East, is especially known for his antipelagianism[7] which has exercised a deep, and sometimes tyrannical, influence over the theological thinking and spirituality of the West We must not forget, however,

---

[7] The monk Pelagius was a bishop from Brittany born in Palestine. He was a teacher in the fifth century saying that man could by his own force avoid sin. St Augustine fought this idea which was condemned by several councils, but the radical antipelagianism of Augustine and of certain thinkers who were inspired by his writings, John Calvin for example, resulted in the dark doctrine of predestination that the Christian East has always rejected. The eastern Fathers have always affirmed that divine grace does not abolish human liberty, a doctrine with contrasts with that of Augustine.

that Augustine, putting aside this point of controversy, was the great mediator that allowed the theology of the Greek Fathers to pass to the West

Rome gave St Jerome to Palestine; the East gave St Irenæus and St John Cassian to Gaul. We can also detect an Augustinian current in Orthodoxy after the schism; as examples, we can note Nicholas Cabasilas (1320/25–1390) in Byzantium and St Tikhon of Zadonsk (1724–83) in Russia.[8] Tikhon was a commentator of St Augustine's writings as well as an assiduous reader of St John Chrysostom. He also served as the prototype for Dostoevsky's literary character Elder Zosimus, and found inspiration in reading the works of Joseph Hall an Anglican bishop and of Johann Arndt a German pietist

Flowing the other way, the spirituality of Port-Royal in seventeenth century France was deeply influenced by the tradition of the eastern Fathers which the *Solitaires*, followers of Port-Royal, read and translated. The Neo-Patristic movement in contemporary Orthodox theology owes a great deal to the scholarly works of western theologians, and then in turn it has had an influence on theological thinking and spiritual life in the West, especially in Roman Catholic monasticism.

Similar reciprocal influences could be cited with regards to the spirituality of communities coming out of the Reformation, or rather the various Protestant Reformations of the sixteenth century. Being solidly grounded in the soil of the Gospel and molded by different "evangelical" movements throughout the centuries, Orthodoxy can recognize, without ceasing to be itself, what was and remains profoundly Christian, that is Orthodox, in certain expressions of Protestant, Anglican piety for example. It is easy to detect in Anglicanism a Greek current that has expressed

---

[8] N. Gorodetsky, *Saint Tikhon Zadonsky*, London, 1951; see especially chapters 4–6.

itself in the hymns translated from Greek by John Mason Neale and in the preaching of Lancelot Andrewes.[9]

Along with "A Monk of the Eastern Church," the author of a remarkable book *Orthodox Spirituality: An Outline of the Orthodox Ascetical and Mystical Tradition*[10], can we not say that "St Basil would have acknowledged St Benedict of Nursia as his brother and heir...," that "St Nicholas would have felt himself very close to the burning charity of St Francis of Assisi and St Vincent de Paul" and that "St Seraphim of Sarov would have seen the desert blossoming under Father Charles de Foucauld's feet, and would have called St Thérèse of Lisieux 'my joy'"?[11]

We are not proposing here a superficial syncretism but rather a discernment of spirits in the light of the most authentic Tradition of the Orthodox "catholic"[12] Church and in living fidelity to the Spirit that inspires the Fathers and who calls us today, *hic et nunc,* to try to find a new and creative synthesis.

The Basic Elements and the Historical Genesis of Orthodox Spirituality

Orthodox spirituality is based on a commonly held faith which assures its homogeneity, but it has also had an historical development. Throughout the centuries, it has incorporated the contributions of different peoples and their cultures. Palestine and Syria, Alexandria, Antioch, and Byzantium, the Greek spirit and the Slavic soul have all in their turn left their mark.

---

[9] Nicholas Lossky, *Lancelot Andrewes (1555–1624)*, Paris, Cerf, 1986.
[10] A Monk of the Eastern Church, *Orthodox Spirituality: An Outline of Orthodox Ascetical and Spiritual Tradition*, St Vladimir's Seminary Press, Crestwood, N. Y., 1978.
[11] *Ibid.*, pp. x–xi.
[12] Cf. note 4.

The contemporary meeting with the West, after a thousand year long estrangement, represents a new stage in the development of Orthodox spirituality. We must not see this development as simply the juxtaposition in time and space of alien and heterogeneous elements. Seen in its historical dimension, Orthodox spirituality presents itself as a dynamic process that takes up and integrates "the glory and the honor of the nations." (Rev 21:26)

We can outline six basic and essential elements, six great currents, that appear successively, meet, mix together, and perpetuate themselves in the vast river that is the spiritual tradition of the Church:

— the scriptural element which constitutes the foundation
— the primitive Christian element
— the Hellenistic intellectual element
— the primitive monastic element
— the liturgical element
— the contemplative element, contemplative in the technical meaning of the word, that is hesychastic and philokalic. [13]

In the first part of this study, we will investigate these basic elements of Orthodox spirituality with the exception of the liturgical element, which requires specialized studies. The second part of this book will deal with the great contemplative current.

---

[13] *Orthodox Spirituality*, pp. 19–21.

I

The Historical Development of Some Basic Elements of Orthodox Spirituality

CHAPTER ONE

The Place of the Scriptures

As we have already said, the divine Word spoken in the Scriptures constitutes the foundation of the Orthodox spiritual tradition. Like Judaism and Islam, Christianity is a religion of the Book. The first expression of the kerygma, that is the Christian message, was set down in the New Testament, the book of the New Covenant, in which the first Christians saw the fulfillment of the Old, the first, Covenant. (Mt 5:17) The Orthodox Church is therefore a profoundly biblical Church. In the sanctuary area of an Orthodox church, behind the iconostasis, the gospel book is always placed in the middle of the altar table, and each time the priest approaches, he kisses the gospel book as a sign of veneration. This ritual gesture has a deep meaning because it shows the Church's desire to be always attentive to the Word of God. According to the Orthodox tradition, Bible reading is recommended not only for the clergy but also for all the faithful. St John Chrysostom, fourth century, said, "I do not want to let a single day go by without feeding you from the treasure of the Holy Scriptures. (*Homily on Gen. 28:1)* All spiritual renewal must be accompanied by a return to this source of Tradition. Thus, in Russia, St Tikhon of Zadonsk in the eighteenth century and Metropolitan Philaret of Moscow in the nineteenth both saw Scripture reading, carried out in a pious and intelligent manner, as the instrument of a spiritual and theological renewal.

As for the way of reading and understanding the Scriptures, there were two great schools in the ancient tradition which most scholars currently identify with: Antioch and Alexandria. The school of Antioch, which gave the Church St John Chrysostom, is characterized by a literal and historical exegesis while that of Alexandria was more interested in an allegorical, figurative, and typological interpretation that aimed at uncovering the spiritual meaning of the text. In light of modern biblical studies, it seems to me that an epistemological reflection on these two ways of reading the Scriptures, as well as their possible coordination, is absolutely necessary for contemporary Orthodox theology.

We must not forget, however, that the sources of these scholarly hermeneutical[1] tendencies are deeply rooted in a simple and devotional reading of the Scriptures that is available to all the faithful. There are many examples in the history of Orthodox spirituality, both ancient and recent: from St Anthony of Egypt's calling, to Dostoevsky's conversion after reading the Gospels given to him by the wife of the Decembrist von Vizine, upon Dostoevsky's arrival in the Siberian labor camp.

The Psalms, and of course the four Gospels, stand out from the other books of the Bible as having made a deeper impression on the Orthodox soul. Certain Psalms which are read or chanted during the services, such as the six Psalms at the beginning of the matins service or Psalm 51 express the desire of the faithful to meet the Living God. The texts of the Gospels, and especially the Synoptic Gospels,[2] have pene-

---

[1] *Hermeneutics* is the science of investigating and interpreting texts, especially sacred texts.

[2] The *Synoptic Gospels* are Sts. Matthew, Mark and Luke. They present great similarities in the way they tell the gospel story. We can even set up columns of texts from the three Gospels which deal with the same events often in exactly the same words.

trated the Orthodox consciousness even more deeply. The paradox of the Beatitudes and the blunt commandments of the Sermon on the Mount have nourished a perceptible evangelical current under the pomp and golden glitter of the Byzantine liturgy, and this is especially true in Russian Orthodoxy. This Orthodox evangelicalism is careful not to identify Christian life with the rigorous asceticism of the Desert with which, however, it has sometimes allied itself. Nonetheless, a tempered and humanized asceticism has often been the result. Putting the accent on a personal and immediate relation with Christ, Orthodox evangelicalism calls upon us to follow him in his earthly life of lowliness and poverty and to share his love of the humble and the afflicted. This was the ideal that inspired Basilian and Studite[3] monasticism in its search for a balance between contemplation and active charity. We also see this ideal at work in the founders of Russian monasticism, in St Theodosius of Petchersk and St Sergius of Radonezh. Faced with the insolence of the rich and the pride and cruelty of the powerful people of this world, the representatives of this evangelical current have sometimes spoken in prophetic tones. With a frankness that minced no words, St John Chrysostom did much to bring out the appalling contrast between the rich and the poor, between the unbridled extravagance of some and the extreme misery of others. He never tired of quoting such biblical examples as the rich man and Lazarus and the commandments of the Sermon on the Mount. In the same way during the Enlightenment, Tikhon of Zadonsk denounced the hypocrisy of the rich merchants who built churches and venerated icons but scorned the divine image in the poor.

---

[3] St Basil's rule is at the base of eastern monasticism as St Benedict's rule is fundamental for the West The Studion monastery in Constantinople was one of the main centers of Byzantine monasticism.

Russian kenotism,[4] whose roots are in this evangelical tradition, aspired to imitate Jesus Christ who "though he was in the form of God, did not count equality with God a thing to be grasped, but emptied himself, taking the form of a servant, being born in the likeness of men." (Ph 2:6-7) It sought to share the sacrificial love of the "Lamb slain from the beginning." (Rev 13:8) The typical Russian *starets*, the *fools for Christ*, and the *suffering saints*, (literally: those who have suffered a passion similar to Christ's) such as the *non-violent* princes Boris and Gleb, have all belonged to the same evangelical current. This inspiration runs all through Dostoevsky's works and is also found in Leo Tolstoy. It was present in the Russian populism of the 1860's and in our own times transfigures the humble humanity of many of Solzhenitsyn's heroes, Ivan Denisovitch and Matriona for example.

Evangelical currents also exist in other cultures marked by the influence of the Orthodox Church. The Zoe Fraternity in Greece was originally a movement for evangelical renewal as was the Lord's Army in Romania. The same can be said today for the Movement of Orthodox Youth (MJO) in Lebanon and Syria. Some literary works, such as *Christ Recrucified* by Nikos Kazantsakis, a great twentieth century Greek author, follow the example of Tolstoy's works in Russia and witness to the presence of this evangelical

---

[4] The adjective *kenotic* comes from the Greek verbal expression *ekénôsen éauton*, "he annihilated himself" or more exactly "he emptied himself." (Ph 2:7) It designates a spirituality and a theology that emphasize the voluntary humbling of the Son of God, his full humanity.

On Russian kenotism, see E. Behr-Sigel, "Le Christ kénotique dans la spiritualité russe" [The Kenotic Christ in Russian Spirituality], *Prière et Sainteté dans l'Eglise russe* [Prayer and Holiness in the Russian Church], pp. 219–236; N. Gorodetzky, *The Humiliated Christ in Modern Russian Thought*, London, 1938. On the Fools for Christ, see Irina Gorainoff, *Les Fols en Christ* [The Fools for Christ], Paris, 1983; T. Spidlitz, "Fous pour le Christ en Orient" [Fools for Christ in the East], *Dictionnaire de Spiritualité* t. V, Paris, 1964; E. Behr-Sigel, "La Folie en Christ dans la Russie ancienne" [The Folly for Christ in Ancient Russia], *Mille Ans de Christianisme Russe* [1000 Years of Russian Christianity], Paris, 1989.

fermentation at work in the Church. Even when the official hierarchy seems to ignore it or is even hostile to it, the evangelical spirit keeps the Church from hardening itself into a formalistic ritualism, a perversion to which it seems especially prone.

Has the Gospel of John exercised a preponderant influence on Orthodox spirituality? There is the theory that, while Roman Catholicism lives by a Petrine inspiration and the Christian communities of the Reformation live by a Pauline inspiration, Orthodoxy is characterized by a Johannine influence. Vladimir Soloviev popularized this notion which grew up in the romantic atmosphere of the Russian slavophile circles of the 1840's. In his famous *Three Conversations*, Soloviev represented the Catholic Church as Pope Peter II, Protestantism as Dr. Pauli, and the Orthodox Church as an old man named John. This characterization, tempting as it is, does not stand up to critical analysis, if we study Orthodoxy in its entirety. We have already noted the influence of the Synoptic Gospels on Orthodox consciousness. In keeping with this, the Greek Fathers did not especially favor the fourth Gospel. St John Chrysostom in Byzantium and St Tikhon of Zadonsk in Russia drew the inspiration for their social preaching from the Pauline doctrine of the Church as the Body of Christ It is nonetheless true that the Gospel of St John has deeply influenced the Orthodox ecclesial spirit whose light-filled atmosphere is the very image of the "disciple that Jesus loved." This atmosphere along with the spiritual realism of the Logos theology (of the Word made flesh) as it is expressed especially in the prologue of St John's Gospel read in every Orthodox Church during the paschal vigil, have left their mark. A mystic like St Symeon the New Theologian, thus named by analogy with the author of the fourth Gospel, seemed to have an essentially Johannine soul; he has deeply touched post-patristic Byzantine spirituality. St Symeon emphasized the primacy of the spiritual of the spiritual over the institutional element. *Spiritual* is here understood as the pneumatic and charismatic element following the Johannine doctrine set out in John 4:23-24. Since he accorded priority to contemplation over an intellectual and active life, Symeon gave a great boost to the conception of Christian perfection that was to culminate in Athonite hesychasm.[5]

Various ways of reading the Scriptures can easily coexist in the Orthodox Church. Such diversity constitutes a source of wealth. However, Orthodox Christians feel the necessity of unfolding the meaning of the biblical texts within the Tradition and the communion of the Church, that is under the breath of the Spirit who is the giver of life, according to the promise of Christ given to his gathered disciples: "But the Counselor, the Holy Spirit, whom the Father will send in my name, he will teach you all things, and bring to your remembrance all that I have said to you." (Jn 14:26) Thus in its relationship with the Scriptures, an authentically Orthodox spirituality will reject both the individualistic subjectivism and the fundamentalist and obscurantist literalism that sometimes characterize certain sectarian groups.

---

[5] The meaning of this term will be explained in chapter 7.

CHAPTER TWO

The Heritage of the Primitive Church

The first three centuries after Christ constitute the period of primitive Christianity. It was the age of the martyrs and confessors, and on the doctrinal level, the time of the Apostolic Fathers and the Apologists.[1] Writings such as the *Didache*, the *Letters of St Ignatius of Antioch*, *The Shepherd of Hermas*, the first *Acts of the Martyrs*, and certain apocryphal[2] gospels like *The Gospel of Peter* and *The Protoevangile of James*, all reflect the spiritual climate of Christian communities in which the memory of the Apostles was still quite alive and which periodically had to live through persecution. Inscriptions and frescoes are also precious artifacts from this period.

Three distinguishing traits characterize primitive Christianity:

1. the call to martyrdom
2. the pentecostal joy and the profusion of spiritual gifts
3. the eschatological hope.

---

[1] The apologists were the first Christian writers who wrote "apologies," that is, essays that defended the new faith against pagan accusations. The best known of them are Justin the Philosopher, among the Greeks, and Tertullian, among the Latins.

[2] *Apocryphal* means *hidden, secret*. The term is applied to texts that sometimes were very well known in the first Christian communities but which the Church for various reasons hesitated to accept as part of the canon of Holy Scriptures.

The Call to Martyrdom

This study will not attempt to cover the history of the persecutions that Christian communities underwent during the first three centuries. Nor will we try to explain the reasons for these persecutions. It is simply a fact that the representatives of the Roman state and of high Græco-Roman culture saw Christianity as a foreign body. We must not forget that the persecutions were carried out not only by a neurotic paranoid like Nero, but also by philosopher emperors like Trajan and Marcus Aurelius.

If we look at things simply from the point of view of the history of Christian spirituality, we note that martyrdom (from the Greek word *martyros* meaning *witness*), that is witnessing to Christ by shedding one's blood, occupied a central place in Christian life and thinking during the first three centuries. "Sanctify God's Name"[3] by confronting, for him, torture and death, seemed to be the normal fulfillment of an authentic Christian life. Each Christian was called upon to fight as "an athlete for the Lord."

This image is no doubt a Christian transposition of the pagan ideal of the hero which, since Homer, had haunted the most noble minds of antiquity. But while accepting this human ideal, the Church radically changed its meaning and essence. The heroism of the martyr was not the result of a great act of willpower; nor was it the noble or paroxysmal affirmation of personal identity in the face of Destiny or Death. There was nothing of Stoic inflexibility in the trusting abandonment of the martyr who by his faith opened himself to the divine presence and was thereby fortified. According to the *Acts of the Martyrdom of Polycarp*,[4] "the Lord stood beside

---

[3] The expression "sanctify God's Name" was used in the first centuries, by Christians as well as by Jews, as a technical expression that meant to bear witness to God at the risk of one's life.

[4] Bishop Polycarp of Smyrna was martyred with several companions around 156. *The Acts of Polycarp* contains the first detailed story of an individual martyr.

them and spoke with them." While many bystanders were surprised and made fun of St Felicita's weakness when they heard her cries of pain as she was giving birth, she affirmed her readiness to face martyrdom: "At that moment, someone else will be in me and will suffer for me."

In addition, the Christian dies without hatred or scorn. He does not throw his death in the face of his persecutors as an act of accusation, but uniting himself in spirit to "the Lamb[5] slain to take away the sins of the world" (Rev 5:6; Jn 1:29), he prays for his persecutors and for the world. The martyr does not glory in his own strength but gives thanks to the One whose power is fulfilled in his weakness and who makes it possible for him to make a eucharist of blood. "This is the best chance I shall ever have of going to God." These are the words of Bishop Ignatius of Antioch[6] written to the Christians of Rome whom he suspected of trying to save him from martyrdom. He continued,

> This favor only I beg of you: suffer me to be a libation poured out to God, while there is still an altar ready for me. Then you may form a loving choir around it and sing hymns of praise in Jesus Christ to the Father, for permitting Syria's bishop, summoned from the realms of the morning, to have reached the land of the setting sun. How good it is to be sinking down below the world's horizon towards God, to rise again later into the dawn of His presence! ... pray leave me to be a meal for the beasts, for it is they who can provide my way to God. I am His wheat, ground fine by the lions' teeth to be made purest bread for Christ ... So intercede with Him for me, that by their instrumentality I may be made a sacrifice to God. ... though if I suffer, Jesus Christ will give me my liberty, and in Him I shall rise again as a free man.

---

[5] Along with the fish, the lamb is one of the great eucharistic symbols of primitive Christian art.

[6] Ignatius of Antioch, (*Early Christian Writings: The Apostolic Fathers*, Penguin Classics, New York, 1976, pp. 104–105) was the second bishop of Antioch. He was condemned to the beasts under the emperor Trajan.

19

The same Ignatius wrote, "Pray without ceasing for other people. . . . Oppose gentleness to their outbursts of anger, humility to their pride, prayer to their blaspheming."[7]

Martyrdom is a eucharistic act par excellence and can even replace water baptism. It is the true fulfillment of baptismal grace according to Christ's promise: "The cup that I drink you will drink; and with the baptism with which I am baptized, you will be baptized . . ." (Mk 10:39) Even though this death is painful, there is nothing mournful about it because it participates in the paschal joy. The heavens are already opened up, and the martyr joins the immense assembly of those "who have washed their robes and made them white in the blood of the Lamb." (Rev 10:39)

Even though the theme of martyrdom has faded during certain periods of decadence, it runs all through the history of Orthodox spirituality. As an institution, the Church in the East, as in the West though differently, has not always been able to resist the temptation of taking up residence in the present age, even to the point of becoming a wimpish and servile lackey of the princes of this world. The call to heroic witness is nonetheless imprinted in the Church's deepest consciousness and has always clearly sounded anew. The long centuries during which Greek, Balkan, and Arab Orthodox Christians lived under the yoke of Islam produced many martyrs. By refusing union with Rome in the fourteenth century, the Orthodox people opened themselves up to a collective martyrdom, to a cultural and political death rather than give up the living Truth. Had they accepted that union, military and political alliances might have preserved Byzantium from the Turkish threat.

---

[7] We find the same call to gentleness and forgiveness in the preaching of a modern Orthodox bishop, Metropolitan George of Mount Lebanon and in the witnessing of certain persecuted Russian Christians. See Georges Khodr, "Le témoignage de la douceur évangélique" [The Testimony of Gospel Gentleness], *Foi chrétienne et Pouvoir des hommes, le Supplément* [Christian Faith and the Power of Men] 162, Paris, 1987; Michel Evdokimov, *La Prière des chrétiens russes* [The Prayer of Russian Christians] CLD, Chambrey, 1988.

In Russian spirituality, the theme of the *podvig*, or spiritual "exploit" accomplished for the love of God, interiorized and adapted the martyrs' and the confessors' heroism to new historical conditions. In ancient Kievan hagiography, we read about the *strastoterpets* who "underwent a passion" similar to Christ's and in the same spirit. As such, the princes Boris and Gleb (eleventh century) were venerated because they did not resist their murderers. Certain heroes of the struggle against the Tartar invaders of the thirteenth and fourteenth centuries are also in this category. After fighting the enemy on the battle field, the princes Michael of Tver and Michael of Chernigov went to the Khan in hopes of saving their suffering people from his wrath. They died confessing their faith and praying to Christ to help them. Even in its secularized version, the idea of martyrdom remains nonetheless profoundly Christian. The author of the *Lives of the Saints* concludes by saying that no man has "greater love than to give his life for his friends."

There is hardly any doubt that the Russian "populism" of the nineteenth century had its inspiration, in part at least, in this ecclesial and popular theme. The Russian revolutionaries of the nineteenth century were not far from the ideal of the *podvig* in that they were ready for the abrupt necessity of sacrifice, abnegation, and total devotion to the cause of the people. Tragically, at the same time, these revolutionaries turned against and scorned the Church because they felt that, under the golden ornaments and liturgical pomp, it had lost the sense of Christian heroism. Less than a century later, however, this same Church was to rediscover Christian heroism, this time in its blood-stained martyrs. During the Bolshevik Revolution, the Russian Church learned first hand what the primitive Church lived with day by day. The *Acts* of these new martyrs have not yet been published, and the present day historical conditions have once again changed. We only have to read a document like the letter of Alexander Solzhenitsyn to Patriarch Pimen, along with the responses that it elicited,[8] to understand that the question of martyrdom, or at least the confession of the faith at the cost of real dangers and sufferings, is still quite alive in the Russian Orthodox Church. We have similar testimony in the form of documents about detainees in mental hospitals, many of them Christians,[9] who opposed the regime for spiritual reasons. Moreover, the breath of heroic faith runs through the whole of Solzhenitsyn's literary work which is illuminated by the shining presence of witnesses of the Spirit in a world turned into a concentration camp. Christ is present in his Spirit, mysteriously, *incognito*, as in the wonderful novel by Petru Dumitriu.[10] His name is not always explicitly pronounced, but he is present in those who have received the revelation of Love, who love man while suffering and sacrificing themselves for him.[11]

At the same time and without watering down the ancient call to blood martyrdom, another form of heroic but bloodless Christian witness is being heard in the Orthodox Church. Alexander Bukharev, 1822–1871, was an unhappy and misunderstood forerunner; he was also a great Orthodox theologian. He felt the call to descend "into the hell of modern life and thought" and witness to the light of Christ that "shines in the darkness" and "enlightens every man that comes into the world." (Jn 1) He made his witness at the risk of being "attacked and stripped bare by the guardians of the walls," to use his own expression. Rejected by his contemporaries, Bukharev's message was received

---

[8] *Messager orthodoxe*, 1972, I & II.

[9] *Esprit*, September, 1972, note 9.

[10] Petru Dumitriu, *Incognito*, Paris, 1962. This is the story of a saint living *incognito*, lost in the anonymous crowd of the totalitarian state.

[11] We can also mention the memory of Mother Marie Skobtzov and her helper Fr. Klepinine. According to some testimony, she was killed at the Ravensbruck camp where she had been deported by the Nazis for having tried to help the Jews. She supposedly took the place of another detainee who was to be killed. See *Contacts*, 1965, #51; Sergei Hackel, *One of Great Price*, London, 1965; E. Behr-Sigel, *Marie Skobtsova*, Formation œcuménique par correspondance, Lyons, 2 pl., course #110, ch. III.

by the "God seekers" of the Russian renaissance at the beginning of the twentieth century, and this message inspired Fr. Paul Florensky, who disappeared around 1945 during one of Stalin's purges, as well as the life and work of the great contemporary theologian Paul Evdokimov.[12]

The Joy and the Gifts of the Spirit

The spiritual force of the martyrs flows out of a confident faith which has nothing to do with the voluntaristic tension or the resigned submission to destiny manifested by the stoic sages. Since the coming of the Spirit at Pentecost, a fermentation of enthusiasm has been penetrating and raising the dough of humanity. This climate of joyous fervor as seen in the profusion of spiritual gifts is particularly perceptible in the primitive Church during the time of the persecutions. Christians, as was said of Blandine who was martyred at Lyons in 177, went to martyrdom "happy and enthusiastic like guests going to a wedding party." The gift of tongues,[13] miraculous healings, visions, and prophetic revelations (St John's Revelation is an echo of this movement) were part of the daily experience of the primitive Church. This exuberance no doubt carried with it dangers for unbalanced and immature people. The Church saw fit to combat the excesses and the deformations of such a pentecostalism. It condemned certain spiritual

---

[12] This aspect of the message of Paul Evdokimov is especially apparent in the posthumous collection by this author, *L'Amour fou de Dieu* [God's Crazy Love], Paris, Seuil, 1973. On P. Evdokimov, see *Contacts* #73–74. On Bukharev, see E. Behr-Sigel, *Alexandre Boukharev, un théologien de l'Eglise orthodoxe russe en dialogue avec le monde moderne* [Alexandre Bukharev, a Theologian of the Russian Orthodox Church in Dialogue with the modern world], Paris, 1977.

[13] The first Christians used the expression *speaking in tongues*, or *glossolalia*, to designate the action of grace on those who were taken by a sudden enthusiasm and spoke in incomprehensible sounds at a church gathering. It was a sort of musical language.

movements such as Montanism[14] and Bogomilism[15] while incorporating their positive elements. As for the birth and development of monasticism, we will see later on how for centuries it assumed and channeled this pentecostal fervor while submitting it to an ascetic discipline. The "free-spiritism" in Orthodoxy has always been a counterweight to institutional heaviness. Russian and Moldavian *starets* in the eighteenth and nineteenth centuries became the heirs of Athonite hesychasm[16] and witnessed to the unexpected reemergence of the mysterious and life-giving breath of the Spirit in an institution that was apparently hardened in cement. After a life devoted to solitary prayer, Seraphim of Sarov opened his cell to the crowds of people that came to him calling each person "my joy." At the beginning of the modern world, he appeared like the witness of a springtime joy that should be the permanent atmosphere of a Church that is nourished by the celebration of the paschal mystery and actualized in each liturgy.

The Eschatological Hope

The eschatological hope,[17] the ardent waiting for the parousia, that is, the second and glorious coming of Christ, constituted the spiritual horizon of the first Christian communities.

---

[14] A community founded by the Phrygian Montanus and characterized by a search for ecstatic experiences. It is accepted today that the Montanists were not technically heretics.

[15] A dualist movement partly inspired by the Gospel that was widespread in Bulgaria and the Balkans in the Middle Ages.

[16] This term will be explained later on.

[17] *Eschatological* comes from the Greek *eschatos* meaning *last*. It means the knowledge of the last things, like the divine judgment or the coming of the Kingdom of God at the Parousia. By extension, we use the word for the last things themselves: the eschatological hope, that is the hope of the Kingdom of God. This theme is developed today by the German Protestant theologian Dr. Moltmann.

Even though the idea of individual salvation and survival gradually edged out the cosmic and universal dimension of Christian hope which the Churches abandoned to the millenarian sects, the cosmic element never really disappeared from Orthodox spirituality. Linked to the intensely felt paschal mystery, the joyous anticipation of the coming of the new heaven and the new earth, of the resurrection of the flesh and the transfiguration has already begun in the glorious body of the resurrected Christ and in the Church which is the icon of the Kingdom to come. This anticipation has always occupied an essential place. For the Orthodox believer, the life of the world to come is not simply a problematic appendix to earthly life. This earthly life is, *here and now*, already open to eternal Life. According to the Orthodox faith, Christ is the Alpha and the Omega, *the One who is, was, and is to come*. With the first Christian generations, the Church has never ceased to pray "Amen! Come, Lord Jesus." (Rev 22:20) Those who pray in this way cannot be indifferent to the earthly sufferings of men. But beyond these hopes, they are the guardians of *hope*, in line with the profound distinction made by the contemporary thinker Ivan Illich. And hope liberates them from distress. In the great saints and also in very humble men like the anonymous author of *The Way of the Pilgrim*,[18] hope is accompanied by an immense compassion and tender feeling for the whole creation which

> . . . was subjected to futility, not of its own will but by the will of him who subjected it in hope; because the creation itself will be set free from its bondage to decay and obtain the glorious liberty of the children of God. We know that "the whole creation has been groaning in travail together until now . . ." (Rom 8:20-22)

---

[18] *The Way of the Pilgrim* is an anonymous work that shows how the Jesus prayer had been diffused in Russia during the middle of the nineteenth century. See the section on the pilgrim in chapter 8.

CHAPTER THREE

The Greek Heritage:
The Intellectual Element
in Orthodox Spirituality

Divine and Human Wisdom

The Gospel was first announced to the world by simple Galilean fishermen, but this *kerygma* (meaning *proclamation* in the New Testament) entered into a very civilized society in which intellectual culture, especially in its literary and philosophical form, enjoyed an immense, almost religious, prestige. The Græco-Roman world was characterized by a metaphysical heightening of cultural values. Rome dominated the politics, but Greek thinking nourished the mind. It was in this world that the Christian faith was to grow and expand in the first centuries of our era. Even though the patriotism of the ancient city was in decline, and the old civic and cosmic religions were collapsing, intellectual culture remained, at least in the eyes of the elite. It was "the only authentic value to which the mind of man could cling,"[1] and only it could open the door to real *humanity*,[2]

---

[1] H. I. Marrou, *Histoire de l'Education dans l'Antiquité* [History of Education in Antiquity], Paris, 1960, p. 147.

[2] It is noteworthy that the Latin word *humanitas* , humanity, was used during this period to translate the Greek word *paideia* whose first meaning *education* was enlarged to mean *culture.*

that is, to the life of the mind understood as reason and intellect. Such life was what distinguished men from beasts. Speculative thinking was considered to be "a divine thing, a heavenly pastime"; it was a reliable ascetical technique that could purify the soul of the filth of earthly passion, that little by little could free the soul from the clutches of material things, and that could give it access to life in an almost divine state. Such ideas had their roots in Plato's philosophy and were carried along by Neoplatonism and Stoicism. They tended to absolutize the *wisdom* obtained through a rigorous exercise of the mind and for many, philosophy was raised to the plane of a true religion. Under the influence of various factors and in the context of the cultural crisis that was shaking late antiquity, this tendency was accentuated as the different philosophical schools increasingly absorbed strictly religious preoccupations. This phenomenon is all the more important because philosophy, in its various forms, was the highest expression of pagan thought. Louis Bouyer noted that "when Christianity was born, the various Greek philosophies were turning into religious philosophies."[3]

The activity of thinking not only made something of a "hero" out of the thinker, sanctifying him at the same time, but the very object and goal of the process was to rise to divine saving reality. For many people, the quest for truth became the same thing as the quest for salvation. Whether it was Stoicism, Neoplatonism, or more or less syncretistic gnosticism, they were all inspired by a drive to attain real wisdom, that is, a knowledge of and a participation in divine reality. The philosopher, the authentic lover of wisdom, aspired to rise above the common human condition, to be delivered from the passions of the blind and ignorant masses. As a result, he could only feel scorn or at best a haughty pity for such people.

---

[3] L. Bouyer, *La Spiritualité du Nouveau Testament et des Pères* [The Spirituality of the New Testament and the Fathers], Paris, 1960, p. 264.

The Good News of Christ broke into a world steeped in this wisdom, or rather in these various kinds of pagan wisdom. It was a *sophisticated* world in the strict sense, and the Gospel was preached to it as at once a judgment, a condemnation and a fulfillment, but the price to be paid for this fulfillment was a death-resurrection. "The preaching of the Cross" was received with enthusiasm by simple folk, those who had been pushed aside by the ancient high culture and wisdom. The message was addressed to all people, Greeks and Jews, the cultivated and the ignorant; it announced that God was *agape*, that is, a merciful and sacrificial love that had come down to man. It proclaimed that grace was forgiveness of sins and a new life offered to all on the one condition that Jesus be accepted as Lord. Those who wished to be Christian had to recognize the Love of God become man in the Crucified One through the eyes of an illuminated heart. In those new believers, He would be victorious over the world of the Powers of darkness. This is how we ought to understand the challenge that the Apostle Paul threw down before the "doctors of the Law" and "cultivated men": he proclaimed the absolute opposition between the "wisdom of the world" and the "wisdom of God," that is, the belief in the absolute primacy of love.

At this point, it is appropriate to reread a passage from First Corinthians and to put it in its precise cultural setting.

> When I came to you brethren, I did not come proclaiming to you the testimony of God in lofty words or wisdom. For I decided to know nothing among you except Jesus Christ and him crucified. And I was with you in weakness and in much fear and trembling; and my speech and my message were not in plausible words of wisdom, but in demonstration of the Spirit and power, that your faith might not rest in the wisdom of men but in the power of God. (1 Cor 2: 1-5)

Through Paul's words, the message of the faith was proclaimed in its blunt, divine, and radiant simplicity. It had to confront the elitism of ancient culture, that proud self-sufficiency of the "old man" that could be seen through the coarse cloth of the philosopher's robe, and had to compete with all kinds of speculation and gnosticism that claimed to liberate man. The simple message was, and is, to have faith in Jesus the Lord, *Kyrios,* to hope and to love in Him, and thereby to participate in Divine Love which, according to St Paul in First Corinthians 12:13, is the greatest gift of the Spirit. The Apostle did not use abstractions to speculate about things but rather uncovered the paradox of the Gospel in the light of the crude reality of this world. St Paul set before his readers, and us, the power and grandeur of the Divine Love as manifested in Him who of his own will took the form of the "suffering servant." He proclaimed the Good News of God's crazy love for mankind, a good news, however, that was inaccessible to the understanding of the so-called wise men of this world. They could not recognize it and thus rejected it, but the "poor in spirit," the humble, received it, a reception that was attested to and verified by the gift of the new life in the Holy Spirit. Blessed are the poor, those who are poor in material goods, yes, but also those who are poor in relation to the false riches of self-justification and haughty culture. "Blessed are the poor in spirit for theirs is the Kingdom of Heaven." (Mt 5:3)

Here is the reality that Paul noted:

> For consider your call, brethren; not many of you were wise according to worldly standards, not many were powerful, not many were of noble birth; but God chose what is foolish in the world to shame the wise, God chose what is weak in the world to shame the strong. (1 Cor 1:26-27)

> Where is the wise man? Where is the scribe? Where is the debater of this age? Has not God made foolish the wisdom of the world? For since in the wisdom of God, the world did not know God through wisdom, it pleased God through the folly of what we preach to save those who believe. . . . For the foolishness of God is wiser than men, and the weakness of God is stronger than men. (1 Cor 1:20-25)

The Cross is a sign of contradiction for any human wisdom that believes itself self-sufficient, for the Cross is in fact the revelation of authentic Wisdom, the Wisdom of God, the *totally Other*. Paradoxical as it may seem, giving oneself to the Crucified One is not, however, a cry in the night that goes unanswered. Through the self-abandoning that faith requires, the darkness dissipates, or rather is dissipated, by a light "that comes from on high." It is the same light that engulfed Paul on the road to Damascus, struck him dumb, and blinded him to the rest of the world. (Acts 9:3)

Paul's preaching was thus made up of two parts. On the one hand, it proclaimed the defeat of a human and haughty wisdom, walled up and closed in on its own self-sufficiency. On the other, it also proclaimed the gift of divine Wisdom, the communication of the Spirit that "plumbs the depths of everything, even of God himself." But it was a gift given only to those who knew themselves to be poor, empty, and ignorant. For this very reason, they opened themselves up to the gifts of the Spirit: faith, hope, and love.

Thus we see that Paul preached the God who is *both* unknowable and inaccessible to man separated from Him *and* at the same time the merciful Lord who opens himself up so we can infinitely participate in him. He is therefore the vulnerable Lord who comes to meet those who flee from him, while still looking for him, even though they may be looking for him only through the wanderings of blind *eros*. For Paul everything happened on the day when ". . . he fell to the ground and heard a voice saying to him 'Saul, Saul, why do you persecute me? . . . I am Jesus whom you are persecuting; but rise and enter the city, and you will be told what you are to do.'" (Acts 9:4-6)

In agreement with all the Scriptures and Paul's own conception and experience, faith is confident obedience to the divine Word that is preached and heard. It clears a path for the outpouring of the Spirit, for the illumination of loving hearts by divine Wisdom, hearts that open up to him who loved them first:

> Yet among the mature we do impart wisdom, although it is not a wisdom of this age or of the rulers of this age, who are doomed to pass away. But we impart a secret and hidden wisdom of God, which God decreed before the ages for our glorification. . . . But as it is written, "What no eye has seen, nor ear heard, nor the heart of man conceived, what God has prepared for those who love him." (1 Cor 2:6-9)

For Paul, the interpreter of apostolic Tradition, there is thus a radical opposition between *human wisdom or wisdoms* and the *single divine Wisdom.* On the one hand, human wisdom is a fruit eaten up by the worms of sinful man's reason and intelligence, the product of his separation from God. And on the other hand, divine Wisdom took flesh in Jesus the Christ and is only accessible to those who have received the gift of the Spirit in humility.

We hasten to underline that this antinomy is not related to the two mental/psychological functions of intellectual activity and believing. What is being aimed at is the much deeper and more radical opposition between the "old man" and the man renewed in Christ through baptism in water and the Spirit. We are here far beyond the mental/psychological level. We are talking about turning around a person's entire life. The conversion is essentially *metanoia,* that is, an irradiant change of heart that affects all aspects of the human person including, his intelligence. Thus opened up. the mind can receive knowledge of the Totally Other. The antinomy is one of the heart, but not in the sense of feelings versus intelligence but rather of intelligence darkened by pride versus a changed heart, one that has become flesh and blood. The antinomy of the heart unites a heart softened and purified by tears of repentance to a humble and hopeful intelligence. Having received the pledge of the Spirit, the whole human person, heart and intelligence, advances toward the face-to-face vision in the Kingdom, the only place where our thirst for the infinite can be satisfied.[4]

The Path of Childhood

In the following passages, Christ exalts the path of spiritual childhood, not to be confused with childishness:

> I thank thee, Father, Lord of heaven and earth, that thou hast hidden these things from the wise and understanding and revealed them to babes. (Mt 11:25)
>
> Truly, I say to you, unless you turn and become like children, you will never enter the kingdom of heaven. (Mt 18:3)
>
> Truly, I say to you, whoever does not receive the kingdom of God like a child shall not enter it. (Mk 10:15)

This requirement, jolting though it is, contains the promise of a joyous knowledge in the Holy Spirit. It has never ceased to echo throughout the Church and to find attentive ears. We have here an explanation of the relative mistrust of intellectual culture which authentic representatives of Orthodox spirituality have often expressed. As a theme, this mistrust runs all the way from the desert Fathers to the young Paisius Velichkovsky[5] who fled the "puffed up" science taught at the Academy of Kiev.

In a remarkable essay, André Mandouze sets out the history of the relations between intelligence and holiness in the ancient Christian tradition.[6] He gives us an anthology of patristic sayings on this theme, and although many texts contain some important nuances and reservations that advocate a reconciliation between human wisdom and divine Wisdom, others express a radical opposition between the two.

---

[4] "For now we see in a mirror dimly, but then face to face." 1 Cor 13:12.

[5] The *starets* Paisius Velichkovsky, 1722–1794, started the philokalic renewal which gave rise to the important movement of Russian *starets* during the nineteenth century. He was recently canonized by the Russian Church in 1988.

[6] A. Mandouze, *Intelligence et Sainteté* [Intelligence and Holiness], Paris, 1962.

What do Athens and Jerusalem, the Academy and the Church, have in common? . . . Let's forget about a Stoic, Platonic, or philosophical Christianity. [Might we not say existentialist or Marxist Christianity today? *Author*] After the Gospel, curiosity falls by the wayside. Let's believe and desire nothing more.

These are the words of Tertullian, a second century Christian thinker and heresy hunter. In the following century, St Jerome, a doctor of the Church, had this to say: "What do light and the darkness have in common? What agreement is there between Christ and Belial? What is Horace doing with the psalter, Virgil with the Gospel, or Cicero with the Apostles?"[7] The passionate temperament of these authors and the particular circumstances of their lives can in part explain the violence of their words. We ought not to be surprised, however, that during the first centuries of Christianity, the most cultivated among the converts, Tertullian and Jerome for example, were often as wary of rhetoric and philosophy after their conversion as they had been enthralled by them before. The joys of classical culture were so great that some converts even put off their baptism in order not to renounce them so abruptly. Mandouze puts it this way:

> For an individual or for a certain period, the outright rejection of culture may seem at least provisionally to be a less dangerous and more easily attainable solution than to try to convert the whole culture.[8]

However, other deeper and more permanent motivations must be added to these circumstantial reasons. These more important motivations are linked, as we have seen, to the very essence of the gospel message:

— the concern to preserve the purity of the *kerygma*, to refuse all syncretism that might compromise not only

---

[7] *Ibid.*, p. 75; see also Festugière, *Moines d'Orient* [Monks of the East], I, p. 18.
[8] *Ibid.*

a theoretical truth but also the very *praxis* of the Christian life, its radical orientation toward the life and wisdom of the age to come;

— the call to holiness, that is, a total devotion to Christ with all the ruptures and sacrifices that this may imply. Are we not dealing here with the necessity of selling what we have, including the treasures of our culture, in order to obtain "the pearl of great price"?

— and finally, more simply but even more deeply, the desire to follow Christ on his path of voluntary humiliation – including that of his intelligence set within the limits of his human condition – in order to participate also in his Glory and to let his Power be fulfilled in our weakness.[9]

We have here perhaps an explanation of why some Christians have heard the call to go to the desert to meet Him who is unique. This call has been heard in all ages but more especially in those without violent persecutions when the Church is tempted to take up residence in the world, in some particular culture. Those who answer the call seek to meet God in the desert by quieting the noise of speech and discursive thought. In so doing, they clear a path for the Lord who is coming, both in their own hearts and for the whole Church.

Having arrived at this point in our reflections, we need to deal with several questions. We know that an immense intellectual effort began in the New Testament period and reached its height in the writings of the fourth century Fathers. The purpose of this effort was to express the heart of the Christian message in the language of contemporary culture, to express its meaning in ways that conformed to the Greek mind's requirements of clarity. But from the point of view of evangelical spirituality, was not this effort

---

[9] The spiritual path of the fool for Christ, *iourodstvo*, in ancient Russia – it has its representatives in the West too – seems to be an attempt to express the desire of humbling the intelligence in view of manifesting the divine Wisdom. See Chapter One, "The Place of the Scriptures," footnote 4, above.

a deviation, even a betrayal? If it was not, what is its historical and permanent spiritual significance? What is the value for us now of this Greek heritage?

Intelligence and Holiness

Various historians have maintained that during the first centuries of Christianity, there was a progressive obliteration of the early Church's message and that concepts borrowed from Greek and Hellenistic philosophy replaced evangelical purity. Along with a rationalization and objectification of the mystery of the faith which substituted metaphysical concepts for existential attitudes, this supposed Hellenization denatured the substance of the *kerygma* of the Bible and the New Testament. This thesis originated in the milieu of nineteenth century liberal Protestantism and was rehabilitated in certain more recent theological circles such as Karl Barth's crisis theology and some forms of Christian existentialism.

Our goal here is not to discuss or refute this thesis. We simply draw attention to what many theologians and historians of Orthodox theology, like Fr. Georges Florovsky, have shown: the filtering of the Gospel through the prism of Greek thinking was not an alteration of its essence but rather a bringing of that essence to consciousness. Such an "awakening," however, required a creative reworking of concepts like *logos* and *hypostasis* which had been inherited from pagan Greek philosophy.[10]

We do not intend to write, even summarily, a history of Orthodox theology in relation to spirituality, that is, in relation to the personal and ecclesial experience of the Mystery of Christ. We will only mention some stages in this development and set out its meaning for the individual believer as

---

[10] George Florovsky, *Christianity and Culture* as well as *The Eastern Fathers of the Fourth Century*, Belmont, Mass., Nordland Publishing Company, 1979.

well as for the whole Church, the Body of Christ, in which all are called upon "to profess the truth in love" and "to grow up in every way into him who is the head, into Christ." (Ep. 4:12-14)

Some Landmarks

In a previous section, we noted how Paul opposed divine Wisdom to human wisdom. This opposition, however, must not be taken as a condemnation of Hellenism as such, of the Greek way of thinking as a prototype, of intellectual culture in New Testament times, or of the human longing for the Truth that saves and illumines life. What the Cross of Christ condemns is rather the pride of the "old man," the blindness of a reason that purports to be self-sufficient. The law of the Old Testament, a law that Jesus came to fulfill, is not condemned either. It is rather the self-serving justice of the Scribes and the Pharisees that is condemned.

Thus the contradiction is only apparent between the first chapters of First Corinthians and the speech that the author of the Acts put in Paul's mouth. (Acts 17:22–31) There St. Paul referred to the altar the Athenians had set up to the "unknown god" and made allusions to the poets and the pagan philosophers. His speech places Paul very close to the idea that ancient wisdom served as a preparation for the wisdom of Christ. Seen thus, ancient wisdom played the same role as did the Mosaic law in Judaism. Through its errors and incomplete knowledge, as seen from the point of view of faith, paganism manifested a groping quest for the God "who is not far from any of us," and human wisdom was the instrument of that quest. "For in him, we live, move, and have our being," according to the Platonic triad used by Paul, or at least by the author of this passage. Even though it is debatable whether the Apostle to the Gentiles is the author of the speech, the text of the Acts is no less a witness to the first meeting of the

Gospel and high pagan culture since the text has been authenticated by the Church. And as the Acts of the Apostles shows, this meeting was far from being a late happening; it occurred at the very beginning of the Gospel's movement into the pagan world. Far from leading to a pure and simple Hellenization of the gospel message, the meeting between pagan intellectual culture and the Gospel resulted in a Christianization of Hellenism, or more precisely, in a revealing of Hellenism's ultimate meaning as seen in the light of the divine Wisdom present and revealed in Christ. The Church accepted the best in Greek *eros*, that is, its passionate quest for the Logos, as an activity and ideal that united men and allowed them to communicate among themselves as well as a means of participating in being. In the beginning of John's Gospel, we hear the ecclesial proclamation that the quest for the Logos finds its paradoxical and unthinkable fulfillment for *divided* mankind in the Word made flesh: the Logos is Jesus crucified and resurrected. He is the Word and "the Word was God. He was in the beginning with God"; (Jn 1:2-3) "And the Word became flesh and dwelt among us, . . . we have beheld his glory." (Jn 1:14)

The Orthodox Church calls the author of the fourth Gospel "John the Theologian" and thus lays the foundation for an authentic intellectual inquiry based on the faith. The human logos is given over to the service of the vision, the unveiling, of the mysterious and hidden Wisdom of God. Man's word-intelligence is regenerated by participation in the Lord's death and resurrection, but is not destroyed thereby. Paul's speech before the pagan thinkers in Athens and the prologue of John, each in its own way announces the immense and crucifying work of the intelligence united to the heart. It was precisely here, and for several centuries, that the intellectual elite of the Church found itself engaged in its difficult task. From the point of view of the Orthodox consciousness, this work is no more a betrayal of the Gospel than it is a marginal activity foreign to the deep life of the Church and that of the most humble believers in the Church.

The working out of doctrinal positions during the patristic period is felt to have been inspired and guided by the Spirit while at the same time respecting the conditions necessary for the exercise of human thought. In the living Tradition of the Church, it is seen as a holy work. Through struggles and painful confrontations, the Fathers' doctrinal elaboration used the language of a historical culture as its medium, but at the same time it transcended its medium under the inspiration of the Spirit. The doctrinal formulations that resulted from this process are, for us Orthodox, normative, and are not understood to be speculative in nature, as Vladimir Lossky[11] has admirably shown. They are rather intended to protect and promote an eminently spiritual and practical goal: union and communion with God, that is, holiness. The theology of the Fathers was grafted onto the personal and ecclesial experience of "the life in Christ" and was developed in a dialectical relation to spirituality. Formed and nourished by this spirituality, patristic theology in its turn was destined to preserve and guide the spiritual vision that helped form it.

It goes without saying, however, that on some points this long process of doctrinal elaboration has been crystallized in definitive statements. On other points, it is still evolving. It is nonetheless true that this work contains the risks of liberty and human creativity, even though these are assumed in Christ. Nonetheless, the nobility of the theologian's vocation is found precisely in accepting the risk with boldness and humility.

---

[11] V. Lossky, *Essai sur la théologie mystique de l'Eglise d'Orient* [The Mystical Theology of the Eastern Church], Paris, 1944, pp. 4–8.

Gnostic Martyrdom

As early as the second century, a philosopher convert to Christ, Justin, born in Nablus in Palestine and martyred in Rome around 165, opened a school of philosophy in Rome. By Christianizing the Stoic concept of the *Logos spermaticos*, Justin taught that the seeds of divine Wisdom fully revealed in Christ, the Logos made flesh, had already been sown in the righteous principles of the philosophers. "For the seed and imitation imparted according to capacity is one thing, and quite another is the thing itself, of which there is the participation and imitation according to the grace which is from Him."[12]

Despite Justin's initiative, the Church was for a long time suspicious of high Græco-Roman culture which, it thought, was too strongly tainted by paganism. St Hippolytus of Rome, end of the second century, thought that being a teacher of rhetoric was practically incompatible with the Christian faith. The Church advised intellectual converts to Christ to "give up teaching secular sciences to children." On the other hand, the author of the *Letter to Diognetus*, second century, wrote, "For in this place, the tree of knowledge and the tree of life have been planted; but it is not the tree of knowledge that destroys – it is disobedience that proves destructive." "Let your heart be your wisdom; and let your life be true knowledge inwardly received."[13]

The founding of the catechetical school (*Didaskaleion*) in Alexandria during the third century was an important step on the path leading to a doctrinal elaboration of faith in Jesus Christ Certain Alexandrians were the inspiration for a contemplative and speculative spirituality that creatively absorbed the Greek heritage while at the same time filling it with a biblical inspiration. Clement of Alexandria, who

---

[12] Justin the Philosopher, *The Second Apology of Justin* XIII, *The Ante-Nicene Fathers* I, p. 193.

[13] *The Epistle to Diognetus* XII, *The Ante-Nicene Fathers* I, pp. 29–30.

died around 230, used the term "gnostic martyrdom" to designate the witness given to Christ "by every soul that lives with purity in the knowledge of the Gospel . . ."

For instance, the Lord says in the Gospel, "Whosoever shall leave father, or mother, or brethren," and so forth, "for the sake of the Gospel and my name," he is blessed; not indicating simple martyrdom, but gnostic martyrdom, as of the man who has conducted himself according to the rule of the Gospel, in love to the Lord (for the knowledge of the Name and the understanding of the Gospel point out the gnosis, but not the bare appellation).[14]

Clement and Origen opposed "the true gnosis that is our Saviour in person" to heretical gnosis. Like the author of the fourth Gospel the Alexandrians identified Jesus Christ with the Logos, creative Word and Light "who illumines every man coming into the world . . ." Their theology, however, showed no sign of abstract speculation far removed from Christian living. It implied rather an ascetical struggle against the forces of evil and the acceptance of, even the hope for, blood martyrdom.

This Platonizing intellectualism, nonetheless, carried with it certain dangers: a tendency toward dualism that opposed the body, seen as evil, to the immaterial spirit. It goes without saying that such dualism is contrary to biblical anthropology. A second danger was the temptation to esoterism which ran the risk of introducing into the heart of the Christian people a division between the "gnostics" and the uninstructed believers.[15] We can thus see why the Church was hesitant when faced with a way of thinking that nonetheless announced the great Christological mystery which, as the Church historian F. Heiler has said, is at the heart of the doctrine and the spirituality of the Eastern Church.

---

[14] Clement of Alexandria, *Stromata* IV, IV, *The Ante-Nicene Fathers* II, p. 412.
[15] The existence of this esoterism is contested by L. Bouyer who bases his position on the studies of Fr. Bardy; Bouyer, *La Spiritualité* . . . , pp. 329–330.

It was, in fact, in the atmosphere of the Alexandrian school that St Athanasius worked out his Christology, and especially his theology of the Incarnation. He was able fortunately to go beyond the school's Platonism. St Athanasius affirmed that thanks to the Incarnation the flesh became *theophoros,* that is, capable of carrying God, because it was penetrated by the energies of the Logos (*sarkos logotheisès*). The goal of Christian life is therefore defined as perfect submission to Christ the Logos. The whole psychosomatic being of the human person is called upon to unite with God by becoming one with the Logos in baptism and the gift of the Spirit. This possibility of mystical union was what was really at stake during the Christological discussions of the fourth century.[16]

It may seem that the results of this struggle, the definitions of Nicæa and Chalcedon, were but dry intellectual statements, very far removed from the concrete personal experience of the faithful. But as the Monk of the Eastern Church has written, thus clarifying the relation between the human and the divine natures in the person of Christ, the "christology of Chalcedon in reality establishes the general outline of the spiritual life of a man in whom Christ operates and who takes Him for his model."[17]

The violent discussions that took place over words such as *homoousios,* of the same substance, and *homoiousios,* of similar substance, can be explained by the concern for preserving not some speculative truth but rather the personal experience of this truth: the possibility of an analogous reproduction of the Incarnation in the most humble believer.

---

[16] "The whole development of the dogmatic struggles . . . , if we take the purely spiritual point of view, appears to us to be dominated by the Church's constant concern, at each moment of its history, to safeguard the possibility for all Christians of attaining the fullness of mystical union."; V. Lossky, *Essai* . . ., pp. 7–8.

[17] The Monk of the Eastern Church, *Orthodox Spirituality,* p. 9.

We sometimes hear statements about Orthodoxy's "Platonism," but the Church, as the one who feeds mankind with the Wisdom of God, is not tied to any particular philosophy. It is quite true that the Church Fathers used Platonic and Neoplatonic terminology, but then it was the common philosophical language of their time. They nonetheless borrowed the words with complete freedom; they remodeled them and sometimes radically transformed the meaning of certain concepts which exploded the very framework of ancient thought. They crucified the philosophical terminology, so to speak, thus making it an appropriate vehicle for talking about the "new life."

We only need look, for example, at the treatment of the word *Logos*. In Platonism, it was used to mean a divine Being, an intermediary between the absolutely transcendent One and the multiplicity of created beings. In patristic theology, it became the Name of God who transcends the universe in order to become, by love, *the Man among men.*

In the thought and spirituality of the Church Fathers, we can also find Stoic themes creatively accepted and transformed as well as a certain Christian Aristotelianism whose most eminent representative in the East was St. John of Damascus, who lived in the eighth century.

Conclusion

The Fathers' "gnostic martyrdom" aimed at illumining the whole of existence. Inspired by their love of Christ, it involved a heroic and crucifying effort at forging a conceptual instrument capable of orienting human intelligence toward the sun of divine Wisdom by enlightening the faith. The fruits of this labor are found in the great doxological statements of the Creed and have been incorporated into the living memory of the Church. These conciliar definitions have become normative for all thinking about the faith that defines itself as ecclesial. They do not, however, exempt Orthodox theologians from the obligation of thinking in a creative, living, but rigorous way. Such thought must also be open to the questions and inspirations of the world *here and now*. It must be ready to give an answer to the spiritual needs and questionings that the world sets before it. While being completely faithful to the patristic tradition, is not the modern Orthodox theologian called upon to set his sights on the divine and transcendent Mystery, and by using new words and symbols in the language of his time, to try to save the world without of course bowing down to it?

The Greek Fathers' intellectualism has promoted in Orthodoxy a climate that favors clear thinking but which must not be confused with a dry and narrow rationalism. This climate is very different, however, from the game of light and shadows that is open to all sorts of syncretism promoted by the philosophers and theologians of "religious feeling." The Fathers did not leave us a purely exterior intellectual framework. They pointed the way to an intellectual activity that is integrated in the faith and not subordinated to it as to some exterior rule. Such thinking is rather illuminated from inside and sanctified by the gift of the Spirit, that limitless fire of Love that burns and purifies humanity without consuming it.

Within the context of modern Orthodoxy, Russian religious thinking from the eighteenth to the twentieth centuries reestablished links with the great Alexandrians. It led to what one of its representatives has called "the battle for the Logos." From Skovoroda to Alexander Bukharev continuing on through Nicholas Berdiaev, Vladimir Soloviev, Paul Florenski, Sergius Bulgakov,[18] and more recently Paul

---

[18] The disciples of Fr. Sergius Bulgakov sometimes called him "the Origen of the twentieth century." He died in Paris in 1944. Fr. Bulgakov is an example, within contemporary Russian Orthodoxy, of bold thinking united to a deep spiritual life and given over to the service of a renewed intellectual life grounded in the Church's faith.

Evdokimov, Vladimir Lossky and their spiritual sons and daughters, who sometimes are from the West, this thought has been awakened by its contact with modern Hellenism in the West. As a result, Russian religious thought has moved in the direction of a renewed awareness of the human-divine Mystery that the Church is charged to guard. Even if the boldness of Russian religious thought has sometimes brought it dangerously close to heresy, this way of thinking is nonetheless a witness to the permanence of a stream of intellectual culture that is sanctified in Orthodox spirituality. As for discerning the spirits, the Church has the right and duty to incorporate into its treasury everything that this kind of research has produced, everything that authentically leads us toward the Logos and belongs to Him. In the words of Revelations concerning the New Jerusalem: ". . . and the kings of the earth shall bring their glory to it." (Rev 21:24)

CHAPTER FOUR

Primitive Monasticism:
The Desert Fathers

Continuing our analysis of the various elements of Orthodox spirituality, we discover that primitive monasticism is one of its essential components. The call of the desert, or better put, the call of the God of the desert, has profoundly marked Orthodox spirituality.

Historical Landmarks

Monasticism is not a Christian invention. It has existed and still exists in other religions. We have only to think of Buddhist monks or, in Judaism, of the Qumran community, whose existence at the time of the Church's birth is recorded in the Dead Sea scrolls. As Olivier Clement has written, this form of life in which people open themselves up completely to a transcendent reality is perhaps an answer to a basic necessity of the human condition. When people are closed up in an airtight immanence, that is, when they live in a world that makes no reference to non-empirical reality, they suffocate. We all need the oxygen provided by those "violent ones" who try to take the Kingdom of Heaven by storm.

A specifically Christian monasticism appeared at the end of the third and the beginning of the fourth centuries. The increasing tendency toward solitary prayer grew up nearly simultaneously in various parts of the *oikoumene,* that is, in the empire and in its frontier areas: Syria, Palestine, Cappadocia. Its homeland, at the beginning at least, was principally in Egypt. The vocation of the first Christian monks was similar to certain aspects of the quasi-monastic life-style preached by some philosophical-religious sects of Antiquity. Christian monasticism differed from these groups, however, as it was rooted in the Scriptures and had a profoundly evangelical inspiration. Certain Christian laymen, in most cases simple, uneducated people, heard the advice that Jesus gave to the rich young man and felt called upon to follow it literally. They felt compelled to follow the Lord himself in his voluntary emptying and in his solitary and victorious struggle against Satan. Imitating the Lord, they went into the desert where the Spirit had led the Lord before them.

We can rightly see in primitive Christian monasticism a healthy protest against a new danger that was stalking the Church, especially at the beginning of the Constantinian period: the danger of taking up a comfortable residence in the world. The birth of this new movement also took place in a collective historical context in which the lowly and humble people, and not the doctors of the Church, were prophetically reading the "signs of the times." Nonetheless, for those who, in Christ and with him, dared to face the solitude and the demons of the desert, the monastic vocation was above all a prodigious personal adventure that God was calling them to undertake. It was a risk that they took in faith and obedience to a divine word heard in the secret place of the heart. In this sense especially, desert monasticism remains a model for Christians of all times.

"If you would be perfect, go, sell what you possess and give to the poor, and you will have treasure in heaven; and come, follow me." When the poor peasant Anthony heard these gospel words in church, his heart was touched, and he became the father of the Desert Fathers. A thousand years later, these same words were to call a young Italian knight, Francis of Assisi, to live Christ's life of poverty in the world. Such is the effect of the Spirit's creativity on those who open themselves to him.

Primitive monasticism was a charismatic outburst that took many forms. It was not a monolithic entity. Nevertheless desert spirituality does contain some distinctive traits which gave it coherence and unity from the beginning. Even so, we can distinguish various tendencies among its members. We can even discern conceptions which seem to be opposed to the path that leads to Christian perfection, even though monks of later centuries tried to harmonize them. There have always been two poles within the monastic ideal:

1. prayer, that one-on-one dialogue with God, *monos pros monon*, and
2. the brotherly sharing of the Lord's gifts as symbolized in the breaking of the eucharistic bread and the common meal, *coena*. From the beginning, these two tendencies have been represented by two strong personalities: St Anthony, the model who inspired the recluses living in the desert of Lower Egypt and St Pachomius, the organizer of community, or cenobitic, monasticism in the Thebaid region of Egypt.

Both men were simple and unaccustomed to dealing with abstract ideas. They were only concerned with their concrete, day-to-day experience. On the level of practical living, both were gifted with great spiritual wisdom. It never entered their minds to set out a theory of monastic life or of contemplative prayer. This task would fall to other Spirit-bearers, to those who at the same time were bearers of Greek humanism with its longing for the light of the Logos.

In the second half of the fourth century, the great Cappadocians, St Basil of Cæsarea, St Gregory of Nazianzus, and St Gregory of Nyssa, developed a more erudite and theological monasticism, which, however, did not separate the theology of contemplation from mystical experience. St Basil elaborated a well thought-out theory to go along with his methodical organization, an organization which was neither stifling nor alienating and that served the whole Christian community. Basilian monasticism is characterized by obedience to the rule "represented by the superior," "service" given to the poor, "welcoming" of guests, and evangelical charity combined with Greek humanism.

St Gregory Nazianzus provided the example of a high intellectual culture associated with monastic asceticism and pastoral care. And finally St Gregory of Nyssa developed an anthropology that was integrated into his mystical theology along with a theory of Christian life that was completely oriented toward union with God.

The Cappadocians were city-dwellers and bishops who looked after the flocks put in their care. Their solitude, in the desert of the world, was fully interior, but under their direct or indirect experience, an erudite monasticism, penetrated by an appreciation of intellectual activity, flourished in the hermitages of the geographical desert. A second generation of recluses appeared in the desert, and some of them, to use the expression that was applied to St Gregory of Nazianzus, were "vessels filled with culture." They tried to express, or better put, to be signs of, the ineffable inner experience by using the symbols of the philosophical language of the period, namely Neo-Platonic or rather Origenistic. The spokesman of the intellectualistic current of thinking was Evagrius of Ponticus, a disciple of Macarius the Great, who died in the desert of Skete in 399.

As for cenobitic, or community, monasticism as advocated and developed by Pachomius and Shenuda, another great "organizer," it was promoted in the following generation by Nil, hegumen of the monastery of Ancyra, and Barsanuphius of Seridos.

From the fifth century on, the recluse ideal seems to give way, although not completely, to community monasticism as it had been evangelized and humanized by St Basil. In monastic centers, ascetic practice also tended to win out over contemplative prayer perhaps due to a reaction against the gross, anarchic and sometimes amoral mysticism of the Messalian sect.[1] A monastic ideal that is only oriented toward ascetical practices often degenerates into a morbid search for painful suffering or takes on an air of competition for ascetical exploits. Those communities less open to the breath of the Spirit were prey to another danger: the monk ran the risk of becoming a mere cog in the wheel of an ideal society that saw itself as separate from the world but from which the spirit of the world was not always absent. Nonetheless, within the framework of Basilian monasticism, as well as outside it, the old personalist ideal of the first monks continued. The tradition of solitary prayer, transmitted by authentic "spiritual fathers," that is, a life guided by the Spirit and illuminated by his gifts, remained alive, especially in Syria and in the monasteries of Sinai. In the seventh century, this tradition was to experience an impressive revival led by St John of the Ladder and Hesychius of Batos who were to prepare the great Hesychastic spiritual movement of the Byzantine Middle Ages.

The Literature of the Desert

The spirituality of the Desert Fathers, like that of their direct descendants, is known to us through the written testimony of their contemporaries. These solitaries did in fact speak to the world either directly through their own writings that have come down to us or indirectly through their disciples who

---

[1] *Messalianism* is the name given in the fifth century to a group of heretical and rather heterogeneous doctrines which relate to the devaluation of work and ascetical activity in favor of prayer alone, through an anarchical "illuminism," a conception of the vision of God interpreted in a physical sense, and a nearly natural light. (L. Bouyer, *La Spiritualité du Nouveau Testament et des Pères* [The Spirituality of the New Testament and the Fathers], Paris, 1960, p. 513.)

piously collected their "sayings" and "deeds" and thus transmitted their message in the form of their life story.

The *Life of Anthony*[2] is traditionally attributed to St Athanasius of Alexandria and is the oldest monastic biography we possess. The fact that there are some 60 manuscripts and numerous versions of this work is an indication of its widespread diffusion in the ancient Christian world. The *Life of Anthony* was incorporated into Migne's *General Patrology* (t. XXVI, col. 841 C), translated into French by B. Lavaud[3], and systematically studied by Fr. Louis Bouyer[4] as well as more recently by Sister Noëlle Devillers.[5] It seems almost certain that Anthony actually existed and that the *Vita Antonii* was written by St Athanasius, but the real interest in this biography lies in the fact that it is an example for the faithful. As St Gregory Nazianzus noted, the life of Anthony by Athanasius presents us with the "character," that is the seal, or the mold into which primitive monastic life was poured.

There are also several versions of the *Life of Pachomius*, the father of cenobitic, or community, monasticism. R. Daguet made a French translation in his work, *Les Pères du Désert* [The Desert Fathers], Paris, 1949. There is also a French translation of the works of Pachomius based on St Jerome's Latin translation; they are found in the previously noted collection of Bellefontaine.[6]

The *Apophthegms of the Fathers* is a collection of monastic sayings and deeds. For centuries, they have fed the

---

[2] The exact title of this biography is *The Life and Deeds of Our Holy Father Anthony*.

[3] P. Benoît Lavaud, *Antoine le Grand, Père des moines* [Anthony the Great, Father of Monks], Fribourg, 1943.

[4] L. Bouyer, *La Vie de saint Antoine: essai sur la spiritualité du monachisme primitif* [The Life of St Anthony: an Essay on the Spirituality of Primitive Monasticism], Saint-Mandrille, 1950.

[5] N. Devillers, *Antoine le Grand* [Anthony the Great], Collection *Spiritualité orientale*, Abbaye de Bellefontaine.

[6] *L'esprit du monachisme pachômien* [The Spirit of Pachomian Monasticism], Collection *Spiritualité orientale*, Abbaye de Bellefontaine.

spirituality of Orthodox monks. In its present structure, the collection goes back to about the fifth century and faithfully preserves the substance and form of the primitive sayings. There are two main kinds of apophthegms in the collection:

1. the alphabetical anonymous collection: a series of sayings in alphabetical order according to the name of the main person mentioned in the saying.[7] There is another series of anonymous sayings.[8] A translation of this series by J. C. Guy has been published in the Bellefontaine collection.
2. the systematic collection: all the apophthegms are methodically arranged in twenty chapters.[9]

Along with these basic texts, we also have the descriptions and travelogues of ancient authors who visited "the land of the monks." The oldest of these documents is the *Historia Monachorum in Egypto,* adapted in Latin from the original Greek document by Rufinus of Aquilæa.[10] In the same category, we have the *Lausiac History*[11] written by the monk Palladius who visited the monastic centers of Lower Egypt at the end of the fourth century. In these documents, we obviously do not have objective enquiries or investigations in the modern sense, but despite certain imaginary embellishments in the style and taste of the period, we do have notes that are full of concrete and believable details.

Although they reflect certain new influences, the *Conferences*[12] of John Cassian, who died in 432, constitute a link between primitive Eastern monasticism and Western monasticism as it was beginning to develop at that period in the

---

[7] PG LXV, col. 71.440.
[8] 400 sayings in this anonymous series have been published in the *Revue de l'Orient chrétien,* 1907–1913.
[9] PG, LXXIII, col. 851–1022.
[10] *Patrologie lat.,* t. XXI, col. 388–462.
[11] French translation in *Textes et Documents* [Texts and Documents], Hemmer et Lejour, 1912.
[12] Text and French translation in the collection *Sources Chrétiennes,* Paris, 1945–1958–1959.

south of Gaul and in Ireland. John Cassian spent some seven years in Egypt and was St John Chrysostom's deacon before founding two monasteries near Marseille, France. According to Louis Bouyer, John Cassian "transmitted to the West the finest elements of Eastern monastic doctrine."

The *Spiritual Meadow* of John Moschus[13] is the last of these monastic accounts. A century after Palladius, Moschus visited the same monastic centers, but the interest in miraculous happenings had considerably increased in the meantime and sharply contrasted with the sobriety of the apophthegms. Instead of being a historical account, the *Spiritual Meadow* seems to be a collection of monastic legends, but if we look beyond all the ornamentation, we can see the solid spiritual good sense of the Desert Fathers.

The Image of the Monk

Taking this early desert literature as a whole, what is the image of the monk, or at least of the solitary recluse so characteristic of the period?

1. *He was a layman*, and this fact needs to be underlined. The great monks not only did not want to be priests, but they only very reluctantly accepted priests into the community, and then only on the clearly stated condition that they renounce all priestly privileges. A monk was therefore a layman who had freely chosen to follow an inner call and live a certain life-style in which he hoped to work out his salvation and to work for God. He freely chose to persevere on this path. It was only during the second generation of monks that public monastic vows were introduced, probably by Shenuda.

---

[13] Text and French translation by Fr. Rouet de Journel in the collection *Sources Chrétiennes*, #12, Paris.

**2. He was a man who felt called upon to meet God
in the desert** and to desire nothing else but Him, and this
without any human consolation, in exterior solitude and
silence.

The solitary monk saw his basic vocation in a solitary
meeting, one on one, with God. The desert, or his cell, was
the space of a life-giving atmosphere where he had to enclose
himself in order to breathe. In the words of Abba Anthony,

> Fish will die if they stay too long out of water. In the same
> way, monks who stay too long outside their cells or who
> spend too much time with people of the world lose the
> intensity of their peace. We must hurry to our cells, as fish
> to the sea, for fear of losing our inner vigilance if we stay
> too long on the outside.[14]

Nonetheless, the men of the world came to the recluses;
they were not pushed away but received with love and
compassion. Sometimes, especially in times of crisis, the
monks felt called upon to go out into the world and to fight
to sustain the people's courage and to announce prophetically the coming judgment of God. Anthony declined to go to
Constantinople on the emperor Constantius' invitation but
did write to him offering advice on various matters. On two
occasions during the persecution of Maximus and at the
beginning of the Arian crisis, Anthony went to Alexandria.[15]
He also gave in to the insistence of some young monks who
were looking for advice from him. Nor did he feel it beneath
him to take recreation time with the brothers even though
the super-champions of solitary life were scandalized.

---

[14] *Apoph.* 10. We quote from the alphabetical series.
[15] "The desert is only a place of passage, and the Spirit who pushed the monks
to go there also called them back, transfigured, to the city of men. Clothed in
his power (Lk 4:14), they became the humble servants of their brothers. We
have here the fertile dialectic of which the life of Anthony is the prototype."
N. Devillers, *Saint Antoine le Grand* [St. Anthony the Great], p. 8.

3. The monk was a wide-awake watchman.[16] He submitted his body and thoughts to ascetic discipline, that is, to exercises – in the proper sense of the term – which prepared the whole person to become, by grace, the temple of the Holy Spirit. Ascetic discipline, especially as it touched the body (fasting, continence, and sleep deprivation) played an important role in the life of the solitary monks.

This attitude toward physical asceticism was sometimes accompanied by a certain scorn for the body and by the dualism that was part of the Hellenistic and Græco-Roman culture. It is not impossible that these two factors had a role to play in the monks' attitude toward the body, especially since in the world in which they lived, the great cosmic religions had for a long time sacralized sex and the intoxication of orgasm. On the other hand, such ascetical discipline was quite in line with biblical anthropology which the monastic experience only confirmed and shored up: man is *one,* body and spirit. The development of the soul cannot be carried out by "ignoring the body; with the body or against it, the soul can never advance toward perfection without the body."[17]

4. The monk was inspired by the theological virtues of faith, hope and love. The ascetic discipline of the Desert Fathers was never a goal in itself but rather had its source in those virtues which became the mark of its power and authenticity. "This is what Anthony recommended: believe in the Lord and love him. . . . He had real confidence in the Lord, as in Mount Zion."[18] The rough and austere life of the desert was thus imbued with a love and personal tenderness for Jesus. Anthony said, "Take great care to cling first and foremost to the Lord. He called his two companions, . . . and said to them, 'Always

---

[16] This is the meaning of the word *neptikos* often applied to monks.
[17] L. Bouyer, *Vie de saint Antoine* [The Life of St. Anthony]
[18] *Vie* . . ., chp. 55 and 51.

breathe Christ.'"[19] The secret of the Fathers' serenity and of their victorious joy in the midst of temptations and the suffering of the world was simply trust in the Lord: "I said to the devil: 'By his coming, Christ has made you weak; he has disarmed and crushed you . . .'"[20] In one of the healing sayings, we read that "when called on in the name of the Lord Jesus Christ, the demon went out of the man who was immediately healed.'"[21]

5. The desert Fathers sought detachment, apatheia. This word is very often misunderstood. It has been translated as impassibility or lack of passions in the sense of Stoic impassibility. But the apatheia of the Desert Fathers is rather the complete opposite of emotional anesthesia. It is the giving up of spiritual avarice, of the desire of possessing persons and things, and in no way implies a scorn for them. As the fruit of love, apatheia is a detachment which results in a deeper attachment. In the words of the Monk of the Eastern Church, apatheia "is, in reality, the state of a soul in which love towards God and men is so ruling and burning as to leave no room for (self-centered) human passions."[22] As a disciple of the "God who loves mankind," Abba Anthony said that "he never preferred his own personal advantage to the edification of a brother." Wounded by divine love, Abba John Colobis heard a piercingly sweet voice coming from "the other side": "Take wings of fire and come to me."[23] Diadochus of Photice was thus able to speak in paradoxical terms of the "fire of apatheia."

---

[19] *Vie . . .,* chp. 91.
[20] *Vie . . .,* chp. 41.
[21] *Vie . . .,* chp. 3.
[22] A Monk of the Eastern Church, *Orthodox Spirituality,* St. Vladimir's Seminary Press, Crestwood, N. Y., 1978, p. 15.
[23] *Apoph.,* 14.

6. *The monk was a fighter against demonic powers*
that, like parasites, attached themselves to people's inner
being and alienated them from their own liberty. Today we
would talk in terms of unconscious drives. The Desert
Fathers were strong because they had received the gift of
the Spirit. These rough and tough athletes of the Lord were
also basically charismatic individuals whose daily lives
were illuminated by visions and filled with the gifts of
prophesy and healing.[24] Nonetheless, they never felt superior to the most humble Christian living in the world. Every
time a solitary monk was tempted by pride, a dream or a
piece of advice would bring him back to his senses. He
would then see before him a model of Christian perfection,
that is, some humble believer who was leading an apparently very ordinary life but who was in fact secretly transfigured by faith and love.

It was given to Abba Anthony to see a doctor in
Alexandria who was simply and humbly doing what God
had given him to do. His inner being stood in the presence
of the Lord as he worked and prayed. According to the
literature of the desert, this is the goal of our life in this
world as it is set out for all Christians, a goal that the
solitary monk tried to attain through his special vocation.

7. *The monk was a spiritual father.* In bringing to a
close this brief description of the image of a monk as set
out in the first monastic writings, we must also note spiritual paternity as a charism proper to the monastic way,
as the sign of the monk's mysterious fertility. It was in the
desert that the idea of the elder (the pater pneumatikos of
the Greeks, the starets of the Slavs) took shape. This gift
of the Spirit was distinct from the bishop's charism which
was also linked to paternity but of a different order, that of
the objective sacramental structure of the Church. The

---

[24] *Apoph.*, 23–30.

spiritual fatherhood of the monk-layman was a personal gift that allowed him to transmit life, and like a father to beget children in the liberty of the Spirit. The distinction, without exclusive reciprocity, and the equal dignity accorded to these two forms of paternity are part of the precious heritage that the Desert Fathers have passed on to us, a heritage that the Orthodox Church has been able to preserve.

II

The Contemplative Element
in Orthodox Spirituality
In Search of the
Depths of the Heart

CHAPTER FIVE

The Origins of Hesychasm

It is generally accepted that the spirituality of the Orthodox Church is characterized by a contemplative attitude. Liturgical symbolism, the content of liturgical prayer, and the importance given to the veneration of images direct the inner eye of the prayerful person to the adoring contemplation of the divine mysteries. Through the icon, this contemplation is opened up to the most humble believer.

In addition, specific techniques of contemplation have developed over the centuries, especially in the Byzantine Middle Ages. *Contemplation* is here understood in the restricted meaning of *mystical prayer* and of *a sensible,*[1] *deeply felt experience of union with God.* These techniques spread out over the whole Orthodox world from monastic centers. Hesychasm was at first a movement promoted by monks for monks but later on exerted a profound influence on the whole of Orthodox spirituality. It must also be remembered that in the beginning monks were, and even now most often are, laymen. Men and women use hesychasm while still living in the world have adapted its techniques to their own living conditions. Sometimes visible, sometimes underground, a great current of contemplative prayer waters and

---

[1] *The word *sensible* in this context is not a synonym for *reasonable, balanced, well thought out,* but refers rather to the senses and what can be felt and experienced on the level of the senses. [*Translator*]

gives life to the deep roots of a Church whose exterior forms often seem archaic and fossilized in cement.

The word *hesychasm* comes from the Greek word *hesychia* that can be translated by *quietness, rest, inner peace.* The word calls to mind the spirituality of Mount Athos and its ardent fourteenth century defender, Gregory Palamas. In fact, the Holy Mountain was at that time, and at various later periods, the spiritual center of Orthodox monasticism and of mystical prayer which was at its heart. The Hesychasm of the fourteenth century, however, had far more ancient roots going back to the beginning of monasticism itself. It was a creative movement, and as the Protestant historian K. Holl has noted, was the coming together of currents, traditions and various spiritual techniques in the fire of spiritual enthusiasm.[2] Hesychasm's roots go deep into the Church's most ancient and authentic tradition which, however, has never been a dead deposit or a simple repetition of the past.

Evagrius Ponticus: 345–399 A.D.

In an earlier chapter, we noted the birth of desert monasticism and the permanent mark that this "call of the desert" has left on Orthodox spirituality. We also noted the diversity of this movement which, even though it was originally a popular movement and a simple response to the Gospel, progressively absorbed more intellectual elements. This was particularly due to the influence of the Cappadocian fathers. The unquestionable enrichment of this intellectual element was not, however, without its dangers. Writers like Evagrius Ponticus were very much attracted to pure intellectual abstraction, and it is not unreasonable to wonder whether there was a danger of confusing such abstraction with the longing for the simplicity of the heart. The intellectualist temptation was, however, to be overcome, and the

---

[2] K. Holl, *Enthusiasmus und Bussgewalt*, Leipzig, 1898.

heritage of Evagrius was rightly integrated into a new and original Orthodox synthesis.

Evagrius was born at Ibora in Pontus on the shores of the Black Sea in the middle of the fourth century. He was a friend and disciple of the Cappadocian fathers, especially Gregory Nazianzus. After much hesitation, he decided to enter the monastic life and finally went to Egypt where he lived with Macarius of Skete until his death in 399.

Evagrius was implicated in the controversies connected with certain elements of Origenism which were condemned by the Council of Three Chapters in the fifth century.[3] Since his name has never completely lost its heretical ring, Evagrius' influence has for a long time been underestimated. The modern studies of Fr. Irénée Hausherr, Marcel Viller, and H. Urs von Balthasar[4] have, on the other hand, tended to overrate his influence, isolating it from other more evangelical currents that are part of the great collective experience of monasticism. These other currents have balanced Evagrius' influence. The works of Pseudo-Macarius were obviously influenced by Evagrius' writings, and in a certain sense, they have also served as a counterweight to the Evagrian tendency. With this reservation, we must consider Evagrius as one of the great ancestors of the hesychastic movement.

Evagrius' very coherent conception of monastic life is found in his extensive works often organized in a collection of concise, very systematic sayings. Sometimes circulating

---

[3] What is condemned here, not without some misunderstanding of Origen's profound thought, is the intellectualist conception of the final goal of Christian life seen as a mental contemplation of the Divinity.

[4] Marcel Viller, "Aux sources de la spiritualité de saint Maxime" [The Sources of St. Maximus' Spirituality], *Revue d'Ascétique et de Mystique*, t. XI, 1930; Irénée Hausherr, "Le traité de l'oraison d'Evagre le Pontique" [The Treatise on Prayer by Evagrius Ponticus], *Revue d'Ascétique et de Mystique*, t. LXV, 1934; H. Urs von Balthasar, "Metaphysik und Mystik des Evagrius Ponticus" [The Metaphysics and Mystique of Evagrius Ponticus], *Zeitschrift für Askese und Mystik*, t. XIV, 1939.

under pseudonyms, like Nil, these texts found their way into the great anthology of monastic writings called the *Philokalia.*[5] Through Evagrius, the spirituality of the desert tried to integrate into the Gospel certain principles of a mystique that had been influenced by Neoplatonism. This attempt had its negative side because it could potentially lead to a neglect of the Scriptures and evangelical *praxis* by favoring "pure contemplation." Some have seen in this "pure contemplation" a tendency toward a state of psychological emptiness.[6] However, an authentic transformation of Neoplatonic concepts regarding spiritual life – such a change had already taken place in dogmatic definitions – was to allow this monastic movement to integrate Evagrian themes into an authentically Orthodox, that is Christian, spirituality.

For Evagrius, the knowledge (*gnosis*) and contemplation (*theoria*) of God represent the goal of Christian life, and for him, monasticism is the highest path to this goal. Knowledge-contemplation constitutes the true theology that Evagrius also called the "gnosis of the Holy Trinity." Any Christian, but especially a monk, moves toward this goal through a spiritual progression made up of several stages.[7] Evagrius distinguished between the practical aspect of Christian living (*pratike*), in which the virtues and obedience to the commandments dominate, from the contemplation of God (*theoria*). The first stage leads to the domination of the passions (*apatheia*) which is the neces-

---

[5] See the section on Paisius Velichkovsky in chapter 8. Some of the most important texts of Evagrius were translated and presented by J. Gouillard in *Petite philocalie de la Prière du Cœur* [The Small Philokalia of the Prayer of the Heart], collection "Livre de Vie."

[6] L. Bouyer, *La Spiritualité du Nouveau Testament et des Pères* [The Spirituality of the New Testament and the Fathers], p. 457. H. Urs von Balthasar goes even so far as to state that "Evagrius' mystique taken in the strict deduction of its consequences is closer to the essence of Buddhism than to Christianity," *op. cit.*, pp. 31–47.

[7] The same idea of a spiritual progression or ascension is found in Gregory of Nyssa, especially in his *Life of Moses.*

sary condition for moving on to the second stage. The contemplative stage itself has two degrees:

1. beyond the influence of deforming passions, the Christian comes to know created beings in their truth and logical knowledge, that is, as they conform to divine reason, to the *Logos* that created all;
2. beyond multiple thoughts, the Christian contemplates the One, the divine Uni-Trinity.

It is important to underline that for Evagrius, virtues are not seen in terms of a legalistic morality. They are for him essentially theological virtues. Everything stems from faith: not an acceptance of intellectual concepts but rather the concentration of a person's whole existence on God as the center of his life. Such faith gives the force necessary for resisting passionate impulses, for being patient in adversity. Faith is the source of divine hope and love (agapè). Evagrius' concept of apatheia in no way makes a person into "a stone," as St Jerome claimed. Apatheia does not make one insensitive to human feelings, but it purifies one of self-centeredness. Through the school of detachment, apatheia detaches a Christian from a possessive and enslaving attachment to beings and things so as to permit an attachment to and a love for something far deeper. The path of apatheia is a pedagogical method that teaches love, and love alone is able to pacify the deepest levels of human sensitivities. As Louis Bouyer[8] has written, apatheia "only develops and expands in love because it prepares us for gnosis." "Love is the superior state of the reasonable soul (noûs) in which it is impossible to love something in the world more than the knowledge (gnosis) of God."[9]

Divine gnosis has two aspects, separated by an abyss, even though the first leads to the second:

---

[8] L. Bouyer, *op. cit.*, 463, p. 213.
[9] *Première Centurie* [The First One Hundred Sayings], *Ed. Fraukenberg, p. 213*

1. *theôria physikè* is a *logical* knowledge of beings according to their "reasons," that is, their *logoï*, that have their source in the *Logos;*
2. *theolgia* is a knowledge of God and at the same time a knowledge of our real selves in the image of God, a reflection that presupposes the presence of the Archetype.

As far as the first aspect of divine knowledge is concerned, the words "logical," "reasons," that is *logoï*, must be properly understood so as not to lead to any misunderstanding. They do not refer to a rational, intellectual knowledge in the sense of modern science. Knowledge in the *Logos* is a decoding, an unfolding, a displaying of the whole of creation, cosmic, angelic, and human, as well as of creation history, in the light of the mystery of Christ. This mystery does not explain creation and its history in terms of cause and effect but rather reveals their meaning, and that meaning is a spiritual drama that contains man's own drama at its center.

With regards to contemplating God, such an activity supposes that we not only purify ourselves of passions but that we also empty our minds of all thoughts, no matter how exalted, to which "physical contemplation" might lead.

> The intelligence (*noûs*) will not see the place of God in itself if it is not raised above everything that remains in things. But the intelligence will not raise itself up if it does not lay aside the passions that hold it tied to the senses. The intelligence will depose the passions by virtues, and simple thoughts by spiritual contemplation. And spiritual contemplation will in turn be deposed when the Light becomes manifest, that Light that at the time of prayer sculpts the place of God. [10]

This text in particular contains the themes of pure prayer and of the vision of the Divine Light, a vision that transforms and "sculpts" the person that contemplates it into a temple of Light. These themes will be taken up again

---

[10] *Prakticos* I, 71, PG t. XL col. 1244 AB, quoted from L. Bouyer, *op. cit.*, p. 465.

and assimilated by the hesychasm of the Byzantine Middle Ages. With the Fathers of the great councils and before the writings of Pseudo-Dionysius the Areopagite,[11] Evagrius clearly affirmed that true theology is an *experiential* knowledge of God, a knowledge beyond all words and laborious constructions of the intelligence. It is an essentially loving and worshipful knowledge, pure prayer, where the believer, in the process of finding God, finds his true self.

> When the intelligence, (*noûs*) having put aside the old man, has put on the man of grace, then it will see its own state at the moment of prayer, like the color of sapphires or the sky, what the Scriptures call the Place of God which was seen by the Elders on Mount Sinai.[12]

Certain Catholic theologians, like Fr. Hausherr and H. Urs von Balthasar, have seen Evagrius as the father of Byzantine hesychasm. At the same time, they have questioned the Christian character of his mysticism. They find it to be nothing more than an elevation of the mind to the level of pure abstraction. The term *Holy Trinity* thus becomes merely the Christian expression for the impersonal Neoplatonic divinity, the Monad. This reproach, however, seems to rest on a profound misunderstanding of the spiritual experience that undergirds the whole of negative theology and with it, an essential and permanent aspect of Orthodox spirituality: an experience of the living God, of trinitarian life as such, which transcends all forms and concepts in which we claim to enclose it. "The exploration goes 'beyond' a Person or the divine Persons. It concerns what, in Them, is their common inner being . . . We want to reach the very source." This is still the call of a contemporary Orthodox spiritual master.[13]

---

[11] A series of writings whose author took the pseudonym of St. Paul's convert Dionysius the Areopagite but which must have been edited at the end of the fifth century.

[12] *Prakticos* I, 71, PG t. XL col. 1244 A.

[13] A Monk of the Eastern Church, *Amour sans limites* [Love Without Limits], Chevetogne, 1971, pp. 20–21.

As for Evagrius' influence on the subsequent development of monastic spirituality, it seems unquestionable. His great synthesis channeled the experience of the desert Fathers through a rethought Origenism and provided that spirituality with a framework accepted by spiritual masters as different as John Climacus, Hesychius of Jerusalem, the Syrians Philoxenius of Mabbug, Isaac the Syrian, and finally John Cassian who was to exercise such a great influence on Western monasticism. This spiritual framework was highly systematized and was marked by a certain intellectualism, even though it was anti-intellectualist It could very well have become stifling had it not been for the influence of the Gospel which constantly broke down its rigidity. In order to understand the phenomenal development of hesychasm, we must mention Evagrius, Pseudo-Macarius, and the whole line of spiritual masters up to St Symeon the New Theologian. The somewhat hardened and unilateral systematization of the experience of desert monasticism, as it was worked out by Evagrius, will eventually be seen as a precious treasure, but first it had to be fertilized and stirred by the great charismatic and evangelical current which from the first Pentecost has never ceased to nourish the deep life of the Church.

The Writings of Macarius

Most of the works that go under the name of Macarius the Great (†390), the organizer of monastic life at Skete in Egypt, were not written by him, but regardless of whoever actually wrote them, they have had a very great influence, and they witness to the transformation and deepening of the monastic ideal that is so characteristic of the hesychastic movement. *The Fifteen Chapters on Perfection in the Spirit,* supposedly written by Macarius, have rightly found their way into the *Philokalia,* the bible of hesychastic writings. This impression is strengthened by the Coptic writings of Pseudo-Macarius in which the author talks about the invocation of Jesus' name linked with breathing exercises. Such a contemplative technique, as we know, is characteristic of hesychastic spirituality.

The monastic ideal set out in Macarius' writings is different both from the monasticism of the first desert fathers and from the monasticism which St Basil and St Theodore the Studite instituted in Constantinople. Macarius' ideal is marked by a great desire for unification and integration of the inner person in Him who is Tri-Unity. Like primitive monasticism, this monastic current insists on a break with the world and on the necessity of silence and retreat, but this ideal is interiorized. External silence and retreat are instruments and signs of the one necessary thing, inner pacification. Here is a text which sets out the most characteristic expressions of the hesychastic ideal.

> The monk owes his name first and foremost to the fact that he is alone (*monos*) since he abstains from marriage and renounces the world both on the inside and the outside: on the outside, because he renounces the material things of the world; on the inside, because he renounces even their visualization . . . He is called monk, secondly, because he prays to God in uninterrupted prayer, so his mind may be purified of numerous and contradictory thoughts and may itself become "monk" inside him standing alone before the true God. The monk's mind thus denies entry to evil thoughts, remaining at all times pure and whole before God. [14]

This interiorization of the ideal of monastic perfection is accompanied by a deepening of the notion of sin which might be seen as a herald of Augustinianism. Sin is not only in the blameworthy act but also in its representation in thought and in the unconscious intention of which the thought is a sign. The root of sin is in the *heart* which for

---

[14] A text taken from "Homélies spirituelles" [Spiritual Homilies] *Petite philocalie . . .*, p. 52.

Pseudo-Macarius designates the *abyss*, the unfathomable depths of the human person.

> Perfection is not simply abstaining from evil. It is also entering into a humbled mind; it is killing the serpent that lurks below the mind, at a level deeper than thoughts, and there, in the treasure house and storeroom of the soul, it incites to murder. *For the heart is an abyss.*[15]

Monastic spirituality thus moved away from the temptation of spectacular ascetic exploits and excessive mortification, a temptation which early desert monasticism did not always avoid.

> The corollary to this deepening of the awareness of sin is both an appeal to God's help, as opposed to a prideful voluntarism, and an intense personal experience of God's sovereign grace which alone can pacify and unify the anxious and dispersed heart. "Once grace has taken over the pastures of the heart, it reigns over all members and thought."[16]

And finally we have this text, the outline of which we find reproduced in St Seraphim of Sarov's conversation with Motovilov, in the early nineteenth century:

> From all over the earth, merchants bring together sources of earthly profit. In the same way, Christians, by all the virtues and the *power of the Holy Spirit*, bring together from all over the earth the disparate thoughts of their hearts. This is the most beautiful and the truest of all commercial transactions . . . The power of the divine Spirit is able to unify a heart that is divided and scattered all over the earth, to unify a heart in the love of the Lord in order to transport its thought into the eternal world.[17]

We thus see that the call to an experience of divine grace which is both spiritual and felt by the senses and which comes out of the pentecostal experience of the primitive Church is already present in these writings of the fourth

---

[15]   Hom. 18, 633b, *Petite philocalie . . .*, p. 50.
[16]   Hom. 15, 589a, *Petite philocalie . . .*, p. 50.
[17]   Hom. 24, 661d, *Petite philocalie . . .*, p. 51.

century. This call will be the leitmotif of hesychasm throughout the centuries, and it will be accompanied by a quest, already present in the writings of Macarius, for a *method of prayer* and *techniques of contemplation.*

Hesychasm will develop around, and on the basis of, the practice of the *Jesus Prayer,* or *the prayer of the heart.* The history of hesychasm and this prayer will be forever linked.

CHAPTER SIX

The Jesus Prayer
The Prayer of the Heart

Concentration on personal spiritual prayer is what distinguishes the hesychast from a Basilian or Studite monk. Such concentration requires a more radical separation from the world but also allows a greater external freedom. On the other hand, St Basil's model of monasticism is based on common liturgical prayer and does not exclude participation in certain Church-related or social activities. The Orthodox tradition permits both forms of monastic life; they can even coexist within a single monastic community. The two forms are, however, different ways, or at least different stages or periods of the spiritual life.

The Form of the Prayer

In ascetical and mystical literature, the Jesus prayer is also called "the prayer," "spiritual work," or "the prayer of the heart." Whatever it is called, it is essentially the ceaseless repetition of Jesus' name in coordination with breathing. Precise techniques are sometimes prescribed for regulating breathing. The content of the prayer can be as simple as the name alone, "Jesus," but generally it is associated with a more developed formula: "Lord Jesus Christ, Son of God, have mercy on me, a sinner." This is the

75

classic, though not the only possible, formulation of the prayer of the heart. Spiritual masters, however, insist that each person who prays the Jesus prayer should determine his own form or content; this should be done, if possible, with the aid of an "elder."

The Scriptural Origin and Basis of the Prayer

What is the origin of this practice? It is difficult to determine exactly the first time the prayer was ever said, but its origin no doubt goes back to the beginning of Christian monasticism itself. The roots of the prayer go back even beyond that into the tradition of the Old and New Testaments.

The *starets* Paisius Velichkovsky, the eighteenth century promoter of the Philokalic renewal in Russia and Moldavia, rightly wrote the following about the prayer of the heart:

> We must realize that this divine action was the uninterrupted activity of our God-bearing fathers. It shone like a sun among the monks who lived everywhere, in solitude and in the cloisters: at Sinai, in the sketes of Egypt on the hills of Nitria, at Jerusalem . . . , in a word all over the East, and later, on the Holy Mountain of Athos, on many islands, and most recently by the grace of Christ, in Great Russia as well. [1]

The prayer of the heart is a petition addressed to Jesus Christ the Son of God and centered on his name which, according to a tradition going back into the Old Testament, is a carrier of divine energy. In the Hebrew Bible, we find the notion that Yahweh's name is an entity that in some way can be detached from the divine person and which at the same time carries his power and

---

[1] Quoted in *La prière de Jésus* [The Jesus Prayer] by a Monk of the Eastern Church, Chevetogne, 1963, pp. 63–64; re-edited by Editions du Seuil, *Livre de Vie* [The Book of Life], Paris, 1974.

blessing.[2] It would be false, however, to see in these passages no more than vestiges of a prelogical and magical mentality. A Monk of the Eastern Church has noted the following:

> The name of Yahweh is a revelation of his person, an expression of the divine essence. In addition, this revelation, this new phase of knowing the divinity, marks the beginning of new personal, and practical relations with God: to learn who and what he is, is also to learn how we must act.[3]

The rabbinical tradition has preserved, and even developed, the cult of the divine name. According to this tradition which continued after the dispersion of the Jewish people, the expression *baal shem,* meaning *master of the name,* designated a man whose prayer was considered to be efficacious. Israel ben Eliezer was such a *master of the name.* In the eighteenth century on the borders of Ukraine and Poland, he founded the mystical school of Judaism called Hasidism, whose relation with Paisius Velichkovsky's Philokalic renewal will one day have to be explored.

As for the New Testament, first of all we must not forget that the angel announced to Mary that her Son would be called *Jesus* meaning *Yahweh's salvation* or *Yahweh is salvation.* In addition, three New Testament texts highlight the primitive Church's veneration for Jesus' name. In approximate chronological order, they are Philippians 2:9-10, Acts 4:10, and John 16:23-24.

We could cite many other passages that could easily be found with the help of a concordance; Acts especially has a great number of such references. The Good News was preached "in Jesus' name"; converts believed, baptism was conferred, healings and other signs were performed, lives were put at risk and even poured out, all "in Jesus' name."

---

[2] Ex. 23:21; Is. 30:27; Gen. 48:16; 1 Rom 11:3; Micah 4:5, as well as numerous passages in the Psalms.

[3] *La prière,* p. 8.

In his book which we quoted earlier, the Monk of the Eastern Church insists on the realistic meaning of the expression [of the name] and on the richness of the nuances expressed by its different formulations: *épi to onomati,* on the name considered as a foundation; *eïs to onomaton,* toward the name, showing a dynamic relation to an ultimate goal; *en to onomati,* in the name which expresses a kind of more static immanence.

The Ejaculatory Prayer of the Desert Monks

The beginnings of a theology of the name can be seen in the very ancient writing called the *Shepherd of Hermas* (100–150 A.D.) in which we find this sentence: "The name of the Son is great and immense, and it upholds the whole world."

This theology, however, was not developed by the Nicene and post-Nicene fathers, but in the literature of the desert; we do find healings and exorcisms "in Jesus' name," for example, in Athanasius' *Life of St Anthony.* The Jesus prayer itself will ultimately grow out of *monological* prayer, that is, a prayer that has only one word or short formula. The prayer of the desert monks was a repetition of *Kyrie eleison,* or the Psalm verse "Oh God, come to my aid; Lord, hasten to help me." St Augustine, who reported this custom, spoke of "frequent but very short prayers, rapidly stated" (*quodammodo jaculatas*) from which we get the expression *ejaculatory prayer.* The Jesus prayer resulted from the fusion of Jesus' name, repeated in conjunction with breathing, and ejaculatory prayer. We can perhaps see the moment of fusion in the Macarian writings at the beginning of the fifth century:

> Someone asked Abba Macarius: "How should we pray?" The elder answered: "No good is served by getting bogged down in a lot of words. It is quite enough to stretch out your hands and say: "Lord, as it pleases you and in the

way you know, have mercy."[4]

Now in a Coptic text about Macarius, Jesus' name is already the content of the monological prayer.

> Abba Macarius said, "Let us not permit the fountain, when the water begins to churn, to spray out what is dirty in this unique mixture, that is, the receptacle of the heart, but let it ceaselessly spray out into the sky what is always sweet, namely our Lord Jesus."[5]

Thus, in the far distant past, the Jesus prayer had already received its form in the context of a Spirit-driven monasticism that was already a carrier of the power of the hesychasts' sober enthusiasm.

The theory that the Jesus prayer is a form of spirituality born on Mount Athos around the fourteenth or fifteenth centuries is therefore incorrect. Its roots actually go deep into the Scriptures and into a very ancient monastic tradition that we read about in the writings of Evagrius Ponticus and Pseudo-Macarius.[6] The birth of the Jesus prayer, as a specific form of spirituality and contemplative technique, seems to have taken place by the joining of a theology of the divine name, already present in the Old Testament, and an ancient monastic practice. In the New Testament, the divine name, Jesus' name, manifests the unknowable God, that it belongs to the radiant shining of his energies, that is, his Glory. The biblical idea was grafted onto the ejaculatory or monological prayer of the first desert monks, thus making it fruitful, giving it a profound spiritual and theological meaning. The native climate of hesychasm is found in a monasticism that inherited, especially with Pseudo-Macarius, the pentecostal enthusiasm of the primitive Church, an enthusiasm that was both channeled and preserved by this monasticism in the new historical

---

[4] P 9, 34, 249a; quoted in *Petite Philocalie* [The Small Philokalia], p. 47.
[5] *Petite Philocalie*, p. 53.
[6] See the previous chapter, "The Origins of Hesychasm."

situation of the Constantinian era. Thanks to this monasticism, the salt of the Gospel did not lose it saltiness. At the same time, it showed itself capable of assimilating and integrating, in a creative manner, as with Evagrius, the mystical tendencies tainted with Neoplatonism and Stoicism that penetrated the culture of late antiquity. The birth and development of the hesychastic movement is a witness to the meeting of the biblical faith with certain of the most noble aspirations of antiquity and their baptism by the Spirit.

CHAPTER SEVEN

A Historical Survey of Ancient Hesychasm

Although modern historians differ on certain points, they agree on distinguishing several phases of the birth and development of the original hesychast movement:

1. Mount Sinai and its wake;
2. Symeon the New Theologian in the eleventh century; and
3. Athonite hesychasm in the fourteenth and fifteenth centuries.

In the nineteenth century, the extension of this renaissance into Russia opened up the modern and contemporary period of hesychasm.

The Hesychasm of Mount Sinai

Being situated close to the Egyptian and Palestinian deserts, cradles of primitive Christian monasticism, the Sinai peninsula was an ideal setting for monastic life, and it was there that, in 527, the emperor Justinian I established the famous St Catherine's monastery. Although the number of monks has decreased considerably in our time and even though fires have recently ravaged some of its buildings, the Sinai monastery is still counted as one of the autocephalous Orthodox Churches.

The spirituality of Mount Sinai is associated with 1) St John Climacus, the author of the famous *Ladder* (climax) *of Paradise* from which thousands of monks have drawn inspiration for their spiritual lives, 2) Hesychius, and 3) Philotheus of Batos. But beyond strictly geographical limits, we can give the name "Sinaite," following the example of the Monk of the Eastern Church, to the piety that had the monasticism of Mount Sinai as its focal point and model.[1] It was not necessary for those who followed in the wake of Mount Sinai to be geographically attached to the peninsula.

Sinai spirituality can be characterized by:

— the primacy of interiority, of contemplation (*theoria*) over practice;
— an emotional warmth and a loving concentration on Jesus Christ

The followers of this spirituality, both on Mount Sinai and within its zone of influence, were convinced that thought generated, produced, and initiated acts. The word *thought* was understood in its widest sense, encompassing not only rational thought but also, and especially, the imagination. The impulses which generate acts first find powerful expression in the imagination and the intellect. The essential question for a monk was not therefore "How must I act?" but "How must I think?". The *logos*, or thought, determined the *ethos*, or act. This was an idea that led to a deepening, an interiorization of the notion of sin, giving rise to the corollary that, as a preparation for contemplative prayer, it was necessary "to hold one's thoughts in check," "to keep watch over the heart," *philoke kardias*. It was at this point, however, that the powerlessness of the human will became apparent. Deepening the

---

[1] The last works of Fr. Hausherr led him to see the fathers of Sinai as transmitters rather than creators. On this point of secondary importance in its relation to spirituality, he was in disagreement with the Monk of the Eastern Church. See *Noms du Christ et voies d'oraison* [Names of Christ and Ways of Prayer], Rome, 1960, p. 248 and *op. cit.*, pp. 100–101.

sense of sin led to an appeal to the Lord Jesus who alone could, by the gift of his Spirit, pacify the heart and quiet the uproar of thoughts and passions. John Climacus later on was to affirm that victory over temptation is won by keeping our thoughts tied to a salutary object, for example, death. It would be even better to tie them to the Saviour himself because the thought of death itself is powerless in the face of certain obsessions.

This recommendation led directly to the second characteristic of Sinai spirituality: its emotional coloring, its warm Christocentrism that contrasted with the sobriety of Basilian and Studite monasticism. The Monk of the Eastern Church has written that "a tenderness runs throughout its piety," a tenderness concentrated "on the person, the memory, and the name of Christ."[2]

Even though such tenderness was not entirely new to desert spirituality, it was particularly evident in the approach taken at Mount Sinai. The writers influenced by Sinai often simply said "Jesus" instead of longer and more solemn expressions such as "our Lord Jesus Christ," and then they waited expectantly for Jesus to bring about what the human will alone could not accomplish.

The classic representative of Sinai spirituality is John Climacus (†649). He lived on the peninsula as a cenobitic monk, a hermit, and then as the abbot of the monastery. His book, *The Ladder of Paradise*[3], was written for monks but especially for those who had chosen the path of solitary prayer, of *hesychia*.[4] He warned them against the illusions of withdrawing only from the external world, that is, a

---

[2] A Monk . . ., *op. cit.*, pp. 20–21.

[3] The Greek text of *The Ladder* is found in PG t. 88, col. 1631–1210. See *The Ladder of Divine Ascent*, Archimandrite Lazarus Moore, trans., Eastern Orthodox Books, Willits, California, 1959.

[4] The word *hesychia* can be translated as tranquility, rest, peace. It also designates the solitary place, solitude. In ascetical literature, *hesychia*, meaning the path of solitary inner prayer, is opposed to psalmody, that is, institutionalized and community prayer which in this sense is more external.

purely formal withdrawal. He exhorted the monks to aspire toward inner silence, "a total lack of concern for all things, intellectual or otherwise":

> A hair is enough to cloud one's vision; a simple care can destroy solitude (*hesychia*) for solitude is the elimination of thoughts and the renunciation of intellectual concerns . . . A simple obedient brother is worth more than a distracted hesychast.

The best kind of prayer is the one that banishes all discursive elements, *logismoi*, and becomes a single word, *monologia*.

> Let all multiplicity be absent from your prayer. A single word was enough for the Publican and the Prodigal Son to receive God's pardon . . . Do not try to find exactly the right words for your prayer: how many times does the simple and monotonous stuttering of children draw the attention of their father! Do not launch into long discourses for if you do, your mind will be dissipated trying to find just the right words. The Publican's short sentence moved God to mercy. A single word full of faith saved the Thief . . . Do you feel consoled and full of tenderness by one word during prayer? If so, stop at that word for it is a sign that your guardian angel is praying with you.

The memory of Jesus, in the sense of making his presence real, was to give to the prayer of the heart its inspiration and preferred form. Here is the most important text: "Let the memory of Jesus be one with your breathing. You will then know the usefulness of solitude (*hesychia*)."[5]

We are, therefore, called upon to tie the memory of Jesus' name together with breathing, to pray the name which is the carrier of energy, of the Saviour's saving grace. It is obvious that for the monks of Sinai, the memory of Jesus was not simply a psychological memory exercise. It was rather an instrument, not unlike an icon, for entering into a contemplative communion beyond all discourse. "The eye of the heart" in prayer can see the divine "Sun of intelligence."

---

[5] PG t. 88, col. 1112 C.

According to his vocation, the monk was "an immobile look, a stare of the soul . . . an unfailing light to the eye of the heart." When the "contemplative arrives at this degree of prayer, he sees himself as completely luminous."[6]

Along with the *Ladder*, the *Centuries* of Hesychius, or Pseudo-Hesychius[7], make up one of the most important monuments of Sinai hesychasm. In these writings and for the first time in ascetical and mystical literature, we find the expression "Jesus prayer," *euché tou Iésou*, applied to the invocation of Jesus' name. It is also sometimes called "epiclesis," *epiklesis Iésou*.

In a famous text, John Climacus had said, "Let the memory of Jesus be united to your breathing." The author of the *Centuries* added "and to your whole life." This was an important addition because it opened up new horizons. It underlined the all-encompassing character of the prayer that here embraces all of existence. "And to your whole life" opened up the possibility of associating the Jesus prayer with all kinds of human activities, an idea that will be developed in the modern ramifications of the hesychastic movement.

The *Centuries* said that the Jesus prayer should be "breathed continually." It seemingly no longer excluded thought but unified and purified the interior person. After having purified and unified our minds by the Jesus prayer, "our thoughts swim like happy dolphins in a calmed sea." This interiorization also has to do with the possession, or rather the "depossession," of things. In fact, the possession of things is not bad in itself; it is rather the "passionate

---

[6] A Monk . . ., *op. cit.*, p. 23.

[7] The *Centuries* were attributed to St Hesychius (†450), a priest in Jerusalem, (whose name has nothing to do with hesychasm) but are perhaps the work of several authors from Sinai. J. Gouillard seems to attribute them to a certain Hesychius of the Sinaite monastery of Batos. The *Centuries* were certainly written after John Climacus because they quote him. They are found in PG t. 93, col. 1479–1544. A French translation is found in *Petite Philocalie* [The Little Philokalia], pp. 94–109.

thoughts" about them that are bad. Inversely, however, simply renouncing things in a exterior way remains ambiguous.

> He who renounces the things of this world, such as women and riches, makes the outer man into a monk. On the other hand, whoever renounces the passionate thoughts of things makes the inner man into a monk.[8]

The theologian-prophet of nineteenth century Russia, Archimandrite Theodore Bukharev, proclaimed an "interiorized monasticism" compatible with the life of laymen in the world. Paul Evdokimov developed this idea in contemporary Orthodoxy, an idea that is a quite legitimate extension of the ideal presented in the *Centuries*.[9]

According to the *Centuries*, the goal of contemplative prayer is not mystical silence but rather the attentive listening to and for the Word. A dialogue is thereby established in which Christ becomes the master of the inner life and makes his will known to the heart.[10] Since Jesus' name is the sun of our mind, it creates luminous thoughts to which he communicates his own splendor.

The *Centuries* also insists on the nature of *apatheia* as not being the absence of all feeling but rather "love, divine charity that elevates man and can make him superior to the angels."[11]

> Truly blessed is he who ceaselessly pronounces in his heart Jesus' name and who in the depths of his thought is tied to the Jesus prayer as the body is tied to the air around it and as wax is tied to a flame.[12]

Among the spiritual descendants of John Climacus, we must note Philotheus the Sinaite, even though the only thing

---

[8] *Petite Philocalie* [The Little Philokalia], p. 102, #70.
[9] On this subject, see P. Evdokimov, *Les Ages de la Vie spirituelle* [The Ages of the Spiritual Life], Paris, 1964, pp. 121 ff; E. Behr-Sigel, "Un prophète orthodoxe, A. Boukharev" [An Orthodox Prophet: A. Bukharev], *Contacts* 82, 1973; *Alexandre Boukharev*, Paris, Editions Beauchesne, 1977.
[10] *Centuries* II, p. 84.
[11] *Ibid.*, p. 69.
[12] *Ibid.*, p. 94.

we know of him is that he was a monk in the monastery at Batos. The *Philokalia* has preserved his *Forty Chapters on Sobriety*. The passage we reproduce here anticipated the *theologumena* of later hesychasm in which the Jesus prayer was associated with the perception of the supernatural and ineffable light:

> Sobriety purifies the conscience and makes it shine. Thus purified, the conscience expels all darkness from within it; we might even say that a light suddenly shines when we pull back the veil that hid it. . . . Whoever has tasted this sought-after light of Christ hears me. Once this light has been tasted, it henceforth and increasingly tortures the soul with a ferocious hunger. The soul eats without ever being filled. The more the soul eats, the more it is hungry. This light that attracts the mind as the sun attracts the eye and is in itself inexplicable, this light becomes explicable, not in words but in the experience of whoever tastes its joy. It is more proper to say whoever is wounded by this light, since it reduces me to silence. [13]

We know of very few important texts on the Jesus prayer from the seventh to ninth centuries. Nonetheless, "this prayer existed, was recommended, and had already become a part of the Byzantine spiritual tradition."[14] The *Capitalia*, attributed to St Maximus the Confessor (†662), insisted on monological prayer. Some historians, especially J. Gouillard, have attributed this writing to a later author, Elias the Ecdocos.[15] We have to wait, however, until the eleventh century to see a second flowering of hesychasm, this time associated with the person and work of St Symeon the New Theologian.

---

[13] *Petite Philocalie*, p. 114, #24.
[14] A Monk . . . *op. cit.*, p. 25.
[15] *Petite Philocalie*, p. 121.

St Symeon the New Theologian, 949–1022[16]

Being practiced for centuries in the Christian East, in the Egyptian deserts, and in the Sinai monasteries, the Jesus prayer was transmitted orally from master to disciple. Monks, and sometimes laymen living in the world, prayed the Jesus prayer but never felt the need to establish its definitive form and method or to justify their practice theologically. Even though many recommended, John Climacus for one, that the actual recitation of Jesus' name be associated with breathing, we cannot really speak of breathing techniques as such, even though they were to be developed at a later time. We can say, then, that the practice of the Jesus prayer remained fluid. To find the Jesus prayer in a somewhat crystallized form, we will have to wait for the appearance of a small text of uncertain date and authorship, though of decisive importance and influence. It is called *The Method of Sacred Prayer and Attention* (Methodos tès hieras proseuchès kai prosochès). The work is traditionally attributed to Symeon the New Theologian and appears under his name in various ancient collections of hesychastic writings. Most Byzantine scholars today, however, do not believe that Symeon was the author.[17] Fr. Irénée Hausherr, who produced the

---

[16] On Symeon the New Theologian, see Basil Krivocheine, "The Ascetic and Theological Teaching of Gregory Palamas," *Eastern Churches Quarterly* III, #1–4, 1938.

[17] *The Method* is found in Migne's Patrology in a neo-Greek version which is often a paraphrase. The Greek text with a French translation is found in I. Hausherr, "La méthode d'oraison hésychaste" [The Method of Hesychastic Prayer], *Orientalia Christiana* 36, 1927. Fr. Hausherr's thesis concerns the impossibility of attributing the *Methodos* to Symeon and is based on critical analysis of internal and external evidence. It is accepted today by Orthodox Byzantine scholars. See Archbishop Basil Krivocheine, "La Théologie spirituelle de saint Syméon le Nouveau Théologien" [The Spiritual Theology of St Symeon the New Theologian], *Messager de l'Exarchat russe* 75–76, 1971; A Monk . . ., *op. cit.*, p. 26.

first critical edition of the *Method* based on the most important Greek manuscripts, is of this opinion.

If, as we believe, Symeon the New Theologian did not
write this work, we must nonetheless highlight the similarity between his spiritual doctrine and hesychasm. This
similarity explains why the *Method* was attributed to St
Symeon, especially in those monastic circles where the
memory of the hegumen of St Mamas remained very much
alive. Symeon's personality and spirituality are therefore
part of any history, even a very succinct one, of the Jesus
prayer. Symeon the New Theologian, then, was not the
author of a treatise that, even though it was systematic, no
doubt simply codified the practices and experiences accu-
mulated over the centuries in monastic circles. He was,
nonetheless, the great voice of the "silent ones," and with
him, sometimes called "the singer of divine Love," the
monastic tradition of the hesychasts in the broad meaning
of the term came out into the open. It is this tradition that
Byzantium received from the fathers of Sinai. Symeon's
spiritual writings used the language of poetic theology and
tried to express the unspeakable experience of those who
"from generation to generation have shown themselves to be
God's friends and prophets."[18] Bishop Basil Krivocheine
has shown that, without the somewhat hardened precision
of Palamism, Symeon's mystical theology prepared the
ground for St Gregory Palamas' later work.[19] Through his
ideas about the spiritual father and the necessity of mystical experience as a means of becoming aware of the mystery
of Christ, Symeon gave a great boost to the notion of "the
primacy of the spiritual," that is, the primacy of the charismatic and pneumatic element, over the hierarchical and
institutional element. The "primacy of the spiritual" also
implied the primacy of contemplation over the active and

---

[18] Symeon the New Theologian, "Discourse" in I. Hausherr, *op. cit.*, p. 186.
[19] *Ibid.*, p. 170.

intellectual life, and this conception, through hesychasm, has profoundly marked the Orthodox soul.[20]

The destiny and influence of Symeon the New Theologian must be set in the context of Byzantine culture and spirituality around the year 1000. At this time in Constantinople, cenobitic monasticism of the Basilian type was flourishing. Theodore Studite was the reforming spirit behind this renaissance, and his influence produced a monastic movement that was marked by sobriety and ascetic rigor. Studite monks were highly organized in communities and were essentially occupied with community prayer, that is, singing the Psalms, and social and charitable works. Certain spiritual masters, like Symeon the Studite who was Symeon the New Theologian's master, nonetheless perpetuated the tradition of the contemplative prayer practiced by "solitary ones." In the early part of his life, George – the future Symeon – worked for several years at various important functions in the world while spending his nights in prayer. At the end of this period, he became a Studite monk. It was not, however, in the specifically Studite tradition that his soul sought its nourishment but rather in the writings of the great fathers of Sinai, John Climacus and Hesychius. It was toward these authors that his own spiritual father directed him. He did not find in these writings a new path but rather the confirmation of a spiritual way that he had already chosen at the age of 14 when he had had a precocious personal mystical experience. This event "dug a furrow in his soul so deep that every outside influence . . . like the water that necessarily swells the torrent of the valley, was to be swept into the current."[21] This is how Nicetas Stethatos, Symeon's biographer, spoke of the event:

---

[20] A Monk . . ., *op. cit.*, p. 28. The author does not hesitate to compare the impression of Symeon on historical Orthodoxy with that of the Council of Trent on Roman Catholicism. His doctrine is a sort of spiritual watershed between the Christian East and West.

[21] Hausherr, *op. cit.*, p. 122.

During his prayers, he was then filled with a great joy and flooded with burning tears . . . Since he was not yet used to such revelations and being greatly surprised, he cried out in a loud, never relenting voice: Lord, have mercy on me. . . . In this light, he received the strength to see and then, high up in the sky, a sort of very luminous cloud appeared to him, having no form or outline and being filled with God's ineffable glory. . . . Finally, very late, this light withdrew, and he found himself in his body outside his cell, his heart filled with an unspeakable joy, while he still called out in a loud voice, as has already been said, "Lord, have mercy . . ." His whole person was flooded with tears sweeter than honey.[22]

All the characteristic traits of hesychast spirituality are found in this experience: vision of light, tender sensibility that moves to tears, and sweet yet painful joy of the heart. If Jesus is not specifically named in the prayer, Symeon certainly addressed it to him as we can see from another text in which Symeon spoke of the same event; this passage is no doubt autobiographical even though the person actually speaking is not identified as Symeon: "When . . . this light appeared to me, my cell was turned up-side-down, the world disappeared and fled away; I was left alone in the presence of the light." Gaining confidence and composure, the man in his prayer asked the following question: "Are you my God?" The answer was, "Yes, I am the God who became man for you. Because you desired me and sought after me with all your soul, you will henceforth be my brother, my friend, and the co-inheritor of my glory."[23]

We should draw attention to the personal relation with Christ that is shown in the dialogue. The author does not hesitate to quote the burning words that he heard and to use the familiar, intimate form of address when speaking to the

---

[22] Quoted in A Monk . . . *op. cit.*, p. 31.
[23] Symeon the New Theologian, "Discourse" in I. Hausherr, *op. cit.*, pp. 172–217. Nearly the whole of Symeon's work is available in French in *Sources Chrétiennes*; see C. Monderet, *Pour lire les Pères de l'Eglise* [To Read the Fathers of the Church], *Sources Chrétiennes*, Cerf, p. 82.

Lord. This may seem to contradict a characteristic recommendation of hesychasm that we found in the *Method:* during prayer, avoid mental images, even pious ones, and become attached only to the words of the prayer.[24] We need to distinguish, however, between distrusting an unbridled imagination, that is, the rejection of all psychological conditioning, and faith's acquiescence to a vision that is received as objectively real, even though it is intimately personal.

Symeon the New Theologian was the inheritor of St Paul's doctrine of mystical realism whom he often quoted. Symeon affirmed the reality and depth of our union with Christ in the Church while at the same time affirming the paradoxical, antinomical character of the mystery of communion. A certain vagueness of vocabulary, which may even appear contradictory, is explained by an existential approach to the mystery of redemption, conceived as deification. This is especially true, for example, with terms like *essence* and *superessence,* along with their derivatives, as they are applied to God and our communion with him. Symeon tried to explain the ultimate reality of his experience, the ineffable mystery pointed to and offered in the sacraments and fully accomplished and consciously felt in mystical union: "I give the name of 'consciously felt union' to that union which is brought about in the sacraments because, purified by repentance and by the flow of tears, I participate in the deified Body as though I participate in God. I become God by the unspeakable union."[25] But this God, who unites himself to us *essentially* in order to make us gods, remains a *superessential* God and inaccessible in himself. Later on, when Gregory Palamas distinguished between God's essence and his divine energies, he only used different words to say the same thing

---

[24] "Do not imagine the divinity in your prayers and do not let your mind receive the impression of any form whatsoever, but be immaterial as you confront the Immaterial One." Hausherr, *op. cit.,* p. 108.

[25] St Symeon the New Theologian, *Hymns*, 30.462–488, quoted by Krivocheine, *op. cit.,* p. 168.

as Symeon. Using a more poetic language, Symeon spoke about God's hidden essence (*ousia*) and the rays of "his glory" which illuminate us. In this, he is very close to Palamism.

Symeon characteristically insisted on the indwelling of the Holy Spirit in every baptized person, and we can rightly underscore the Christocentric nature of his piety, of his "deeply tender feelings" for Jesus, as the Monk of the Eastern Church has said. But this intimate relation with Christ was for him inseparable from the living experience of the gift of the Holy Spirit. Even though Symeon loved Christ deeply, he was also the herald, the announcer, of the outpouring of the Holy Spirit which he called upon all baptized people to make real in their lives. We must take possession of the Spirit whom we have received in baptism so as to become conscious, in him, of the fact that we have truly been reclothed by Christ In his catechetical instructions, Symeon the hegumen of St Mamas never tired of exhorting his listeners to "become conscious of these things." His doctrine stated that "mystical experience is necessary for everyone" and was essentially a call to take personal possession of grace and an insistence on illumination by the Spirit. Every Christian, by virtue of his baptism, is called upon to aspire to this illumination. Symeon proclaimed that eternal life begins *here and now* and that we must know it and gain knowledge of it through experience.

"If we claim that all this is accomplished in a hidden and unconscious way, so that we are not in the slightest way aware of what has happened, then what makes us different from dead bodies?"[26] Now in the Holy Spirit, we are called upon to be alive; in him we are united to Christ and assured of our redemption: "How do you know, my dear friend in Christ, that you will be like him?" The friend: "From the Spirit . . . whom he has communicated to us. It is from him that we receive the knowledge that we are God's

---

[26] Hausherr, *op. cit.*, p. 206.

children, that God himself is in us. He has told me this by his secret voice."[27]

The epicletic and charismatic character of Symeon's spirituality, his confidence of the direct inspiration of the Spirit which is accessible to all Christians, has led certain Roman Catholic exegetes to speak about Symeon's "Protestantism."[28] However, Symeon was far from denying the objective reality of sacramental grace; he in fact insisted on it. His call was to a permanent conversion of the heart which alone permits a Christian to harvest spiritual fruit. When, in the name of humility, detractors reproached him for aspiring to graces too high for him, Symeon very explicitly referred to the Apostle Paul whom he wanted to imitate:

> The great voice of Paul himself tells us: "Christ came to save sinners of whom I am the first." (1 Tim 1:15) Here then is the first among sinners to be saved. Let yourself become the second, the third; become the tenth. Become, if you want, the imitator of thousands; put yourself on the same level as Paul and you will honor him who said, "Be imitators of me as I am of Christ."[29] (1 Cor 11:1)

Humbly assured of God's gift, of the grace of the Holy Spirit received in baptism, the believer is called upon to run out ahead, to meet the God who comes toward him. This is the conviction that Symeon wanted to share, and so he gave this exhortation: "The seal of the Holy Spirit is given to the faithful from this very moment. . . . Enlivened by this faith, run so as to attain the goal . . . knock until someone opens the door for you and you enter into the bridal chamber where you will contemplate the bridegroom."[30]

Symeon's pentecostal preaching caused a wave of spiritual enthusiasm and announced hesychasm, but only a small group of disciples understood what he was saying. Most of

---

[27] Symeon the New Theologian, "Discourse" in I. Hausherr, *op. cit.*, p. 197.
[28] This is especially the case for Fr. Hausherr.
[29] Symeon the New Theologian, "Discourse" in I. Hausherr, *op. cit.*, p. 184.
[30] *Ibid.*, p. 207.

his contemporaries missed the point. Throughout his life, St Symeon encountered opposition from the "blind and the deaf" who used the pretext of asceticism and humility to attack his mystical doctrine. Basilian and Studite circles rejected him. Faced with the hostility of the hierarchy, he was called to appear before the patriarch and the synod who in 1009 forced him to renounce his charge as hegumen of St Mamas. He withdrew but did not give way on the essential elements of his doctrine. He remained strong in his convictions, never ceasing to proclaim the primacy of the spiritual, that is, of the Spirit over hardened institutions. He was rehabilitated by the patriarch but never went back to St Mamas. He died on March 12, 1022, surrounded by a small group of friends.[31] His call, however, has never ceased to re-echo in the heart of oriental monasticism.

The *Method*

For many centuries, the famous *Method of Sacred Prayer and Attention* was attributed to Symeon the New Theologian, but it no doubt belongs to a later period. In the present state of our knowledge on the subject, we cannot determine with any certainty the author or the date when it was written. This is the conclusion Fr. Hausherr arrived at after his very detailed study. One plausible hypothesis, put forward by this eminent Byzantine scholar, attributes the redaction of the *Method* to the monk Nicetas who lived during the fourteenth century and was one of Gregory Palamas' masters. Whoever he was, the editor of the *Method*, with a certain pretension of producing a "scientific" work, no doubt simply reported the

---

[31] Symeon's disciple, Nicetas Stathatos, wrote his biography (PG 120); it has been published in a French translation with an introduction, by I. Hausherr and G. Horn, "Un grand mystique byzantin: vie de Symeon le Nouveau Théologien" [A Great Byzantine Mystic: the Life of Symeon the New Theologian], *Orientalia Christiana* XII, #45, 1928.

practices already known in the monastic circles in which the Sinai fathers were seen as carriers of an earlier tradition.

We cannot reproduce the entire text of the *Method* and so will limit ourselves to summarizing its main points.

The work opens with a warning against the errors and seductions of the imagination to which the virtue of sobriety (*nepsis*) is opposed. It distinguishes three forms of prayer; the reader is then asked to choose the best one.

1. The first consists of forcing our attention by "thinking divine concepts and imagining heavenly beauties."[32] This kind of prayer, however, if practiced to excess and in solitude, can create hallucinations and lead to mental unbalance.

2. A second way of attaining a state of attentive prayer is by violently resisting evil thoughts. This method involves the forceful exercise of the will and is fraught with many problems. Antedating depth psychology by several centuries, the *Method* makes the following comparison: a man who struggles in this way is like someone who fights "in the night...because of the darkness of his mind." "Being either crushed by his adversaries or surprised by vain glory . . . , he endures the pain of battle but is frustrated by not winning the reward."

3. Finally, there is a third way which seems to be the safeSt It first of all requires obedience, an obedience "which liberates those who love it from the entanglements of this present evil age," and assumes that those who choose this way will "keep watch over their hearts." Such watchfulness will then allow them to acquire the rest *without pain.*[33]

---

[32] Hausherr, *op. cit.*, pp. 151 ff.

[33] The italics are the author's. In certain Roman Catholic circles, this expression is used to accuse the hesychastic method of prayer of being quietist or even amoral. The accent is put rather on the confident abandonment of oneself to Christ, to his grace of which the divine name is the sacrament. It does not seem impossible to us to relate the hesychastic way to the "little way" of St Theresa of Lisieux.

Here is the central passage of the *Method:*

> Sit down in your peaceful cell . . . and do what I tell you:
> close the door and lift your mind above every vain and
> temporal object. Then lower your head onto your chest, look
> toward the middle of your stomach, restrict your breathing
> . . . so as to make breathing difficult, and in you mind try to
> find the place of the heart. . . . At first, you will only find
> pain and darkness . . . but if you persevere, you will find a
> boundless happiness. From then on, as soon as a bad
> thought comes into your head and even before it is complete
> and takes shape, it is attacked and destroyed by the invo-
> cation of Jesus Christ. . . . As for the rest, you will learn it
> with God's help by holding Jesus in your heart. Sit down in
> your cell, so it is said, and it [the invocation] will teach you
> all things.[34]

The technical and psychosomatic aspect of this method
can be a little disconcerting; it makes the Jesus prayer seem
to be a kind of Christian yoga. We cannot help noting the
similarities between this method and other procedures of
mental concentration used in other religions. A form of
psychic training is therefore useful in promoting the desire to
have communion with Jesus.

Later on, we will come back to the meaning and relative
importance that the spiritual masters of the Jesus prayer
have given to the corporal techniques proposed by the
Method, but let us now make clear that we are not dealing
here with the conditioning or the setting up of a psychical
mechanism. The goal sought after is the liberation of a spiritual dynamism, with the help of bodily positions "seen as
crutches." In a appendix to his work, the Monk of the Eastern
Church set out very important indications on these "psychophysiological" procedures. He said that we must keep the
mind "within the limits of the body" . . . and keep it from
being diverted and dispersed in things. This dispersion is the
result of exercising visual, tactile and locomotor functions. If
we hold our breath and at the same time remain very still

---

[34] Hausherr, *op. cit.*, pp. 164–65.

with our eyes closed or lowered, and if this bodily position is accompanied by a psychological attitude that "brings the mind back within the body" and does not go beyond the limits of the body, then this operation . . . produces an uneasy feeling, which can become painful, but also it is a feeling "that the mind and the body have intimately come together in an intense concentration."[35]

As for looking intensely at the center of the body, an exercise that the adversaries of hesychasm have often called "omphaloscopy," that is "navel gazing," we can explain it in the following way: the perception we have of ourselves as a psychosomatic unity differs according to the part of the body on which we fix our attention. When at prayer, a hesychast concentrates his look, his attention, on his physical heart or intestines. By doing this, he becomes conscious of the center of his personal life which is not found in the brain where intellectual powers and the stimulations of the exterior world intersect. His consciousness is rather concentrated in his unfathomable depths from which spring up thoughts, feelings, and impulses of the will. The physical heart is the symbol of these "unfathomable depths." We need to throw our "intellectual" thoughts into the furnace of the spiritual heart where they can be heated up and burst into flame; then the burning cry will spring forth and rise toward Jesus the God-Man. This is in fact the meaning of the search for the "place of the heart."

In order to situate the *Method* in its spiritual context, we must not forget a passage from *The Letter of Pseudo-Chrysostom to Monks* which could well date from the same period as the *Method*: "When at prayer, repeat morning and night 'Lord Jesus Christ, Son of God, have mercy on us.' Do this even when eating and drinking. . . . Our heart must

---

[35] A Monk . . ., *op. cit.*, pp. 105 ff. See also, A. Bloom, Metropolitan of Sourozh, "Contemplation et Ascèse" [Contemplation and Ascesis], *Etudes carmélitaines* #4; E. Behr-Sigel, "La prière de Jésus" [The Jesus Prayer] in *Douloureuse Joie* [Painful Joy], pp. 103–106.

absorb the Lord and the Lord must absorb our heart so that the two can become one." And then follows the author's exhortation which removes us far away from any crude interpretation of psychophysiological techniques: "You are the Temple; do not seek after a physical place."[36]

The Jesus Prayer on Mount Athos during the Fourteenth and Fifteenth Centuries

The Jesus prayer was certainly known in the monasteries and hermitages of the Holy Mountain well before the fourteenth century when, after a period of torpor and decadence, *the prayer* entered into a period of brilliant renewal. It was the arrival of a great spiritual master, Gregory of Sinai (†1346), that renewed the flame of contemplative prayer on Mount Athos. From that moment on, the Holy Mountain became the center of practice and diffusion for the prayer of the heart. Even though it was to lose some of its spontaneity on Athos, this prayer found its classical form. It would be wrong, however, to think that this classical form was unalterable. The prayer also provoked theological research and a debate in which Gregory Palamas was the spokesman and protagonist.

A certain tendency toward standardization of practice on Mount Athos did not, however, hinder the development of personal spiritual paths. A treatise by Gregory of Sinai, *On the Contemplative Life and the Two Ways of Prayer*[37], opened up the possibility of a eucharistic use of Jesus' name. Gregory said that by pronouncing Jesus' name, we feed on it; it becomes our nourishment. He also tried to give to each word of the prayer, "Lord Jesus Christ, Son of God, have mercy on me," its full meaning. In Gregory's treatise, the verbal form of the prayer was in no way rigidly fixed.

---

[36] A Monk . . . *op. cit.,* p. 36; PG t. 60 col. 752–755.
[37] PG t. 150, co. 1314–1330.

Another spiritual master, Maximus of Kausokalybe, tied the "memory of Jesus" to that of Mary, the Mother of God. In his reflection, Maximus insisted on the unification of the mind brought about by the prayer. Another Athonite, Theoleptus of Philadelphia, assigned a specific role to each of our mental faculties during the prayer of the heart: discursive intelligence (*dianoïa*), reason (*noûs*), and spirit (*pneuma*). Far from destroying reflective thinking, contemplation nourished it and made it bear fruit. Gregory Palamas' theology offered the most striking example of this cross fertilization.

Gregory Palamas (1296–1359) was at the center of the fourteenth century controversies that opposed the Greeks and the Latins. In the twentieth century, the renewal of Orthodox theology in the Russian emigration as well as the neopatristic movement, associated as they are with Georges Florovsky, Vladimir Lossky, Basil Krivocheine, and John Meyendorff, have given this controversy a new importance in ecumenical dialogue. As the same time, these theologians have renewed the discussion on the fundamental elements of the question.[38]

An analysis of Gregory's doctrine would go beyond the limits of this brief historical outline. Suffice it to say that Gregory Palamas followed the hesychastic way during his stay in several monasteries of Mount Athos. When Barlaam, a monk from Calabria in southern Italy, launched an attack against the hesychastic monks calling them heretics, Massalians,

---

[38] The traditional Catholic theses on the "Palamite heresy" are found in Fr. Jugie, "Palamas" and "Controverse palamite," *Dictionnaire de théologie catholique* XI, Vacant et Mangenot, Paris, 1931. These articles are well documented but have no sympathy for St. Gregory. Among the Orthodox works on Palamas see the following: Basil Krivocheine, "The Ascetic and Theological Teaching of Gregory Palamas," *Eastern Churches Quarterly* III, #1–4, 1938; V. Lossky, *The Mystical Theology of the Eastern Church,* Fellowship of St. Alban and St. Sergius, London, 1957; Lossky, "La Théologie de la lumière chez Grégoire de Thessalonique" [The Theology of Light in Gregory of Thessalonica], *Dieu Vivant* #1, 1946; Fr. John Meyendorff, *A Study of Gregory Palamas,* The Faith Press, Aylesbury, England, 1974 and *St. Gregory Palamas and Orthodox Spirituality,* St. Vladimir's Press, Crestwood, N. Y., 1974.

and "navel gazers,"[39] Gregory defended them, and from then on, he became embroiled in a fiery struggle. In Gregory's works, there is hardly any explicit mention of the Jesus prayer, but it is at all times in the background because the monks Gregory defended were the very ones who practiced it. His famous distinction between God's unknowable essence and his energies in which we can participate was destined to preserve the contemplative monks' experience of communion with Christ, and this without in any way diminishing God's absolute transcendence. In the same way, the affirmation of the uncreated character of the "Light of Tabor" aimed at expressing the ineffable mystery of a transcendent God who bestows his grace and thus gives himself to those who invoke his name with faith and love. It is certainly regrettable, as the Monk of the Eastern Church has said, that "a current of simple and tender piety became in the fourteenth century a flood of quarrels" which were aggravated by misunderstandings on both sides. We must, nonetheless, understand that the quarrel was not simply over words. Gregory Palamas was defending the integrity of the Christian mystery and the authenticity of the mystics' spiritual experience.

Gregory's personal destiny was quite agitated. He was imprisoned, excommunicated, rehabilitated, and promoted to be archbishop of Thessalonica. He was exiled once again and captured by Turkish pirates. In 1355, his doctrine was declared the official doctrine of the Byzantine Church. In 1341, the abbots along with the most important monks of Mount Athos declared themselves in favor of Gregory Palamas in a document called *The Hagioritic Tome*, and less than ten years after his death, he was canonized by the Orthodox Church. By forcefully affirming the full reality of deification, to which man in his psychosomatic wholeness is called,

---

[39] This is name-calling that refers to the advice found in *The Method* saying that those who pray the Jesus prayer should look at the middle of the bodies, that is, the navel.

Palamism completed the work of the great councils of the fourth and fifth centuries. Fr. John Meyendorff has written that "the victory of Palamas was the victory of Christian humanism over the pagan humanism of the Renaissance."[40] Having been first won on the doctrinal level, this victory must take root in the lives of the faithful, in the personal and social dimension of a eucharistic existence. According to a modern Orthodox theologian, A. M. Bukharev, it is the task of the Orthodox Church to proclaim this message in the contemporary world, a task that must be carried out in creative faithfulness to the hesychasts' message.[41]

From Mount Athos in the fourteenth and fifteenth centuries, the Jesus prayer spread out to the Greek, Slavic, and Moldavian EaSt Historical documents mention the fact that in Russia the disciples of St Sergius of Radonezh (1314–1392) used the prayer, and it is possible that St Sergius himself used it. Certainly, his luminous visions and inclination toward the solitary life allow us to associate him with the hesychasts.[42] In the fifteenth century, Nil Sorsky and the "startsi beyond the Volga" seem to have been zealous advocates of the prayer of the heart. Their ideal of evangelical poverty and spiritual liberty set them against the hardened institutionalism and ritualism that, with Joseph of Volokolamsk, was to prevail in the official circles of the Russian Church from the sixteenth century on.[43] This

---

[40] J. Meyendorff, St Gregory Palamas . . ., p. 174.

[41] Behr-Sigel, Alexandre Bukharev, pp. 96–97.

[42] On St Sergius of Radonezh, see P. Kovalevsky, Saint Serge et la spiritualité russe [St Sergius and Russian Spirituality], Paris, 1958.

[43] On the contemplative stream allied to anchoritic monasticism of ancient Russia, see, E. Behr-Sigel, Prière et Sainteté dans l'Eglise russe [Prayer and Holiness in the Russian Church]. On Nil Sorsky, see George Maloney, La Spiritualité de Nil Sorsky [The Spirituality of Nil Sorsky], Bellefontaine, 1980; E. Behr-Sigel, "Nil Sorsky, un hésychaste lettré" [Nil Sorsky a Learned Hesychast], in Monachisme d'Orient et d'Occident [Eastern and Western Monasticism], L'Association des amis de Sénanque, 1987. The history of hesychasm in the areas that now constitute Romania has been studied by Romul Joanta, Roumanie: tradition et culture hésychastes [Romania: Hesychastic Tradition and Culture], Bellefontaine, 1987.

underground current of evangelical and charismatic piety, however, never dried up completely. It was nourished on the Jesus prayer, and in the second half of the eighteenth century, the century of the Enlightenment, it experienced, with the *starets* Paisius, an amazing renaissance.

CHAPTER EIGHT

The Philokalic Renaissance and Its Spread into Russia

The *Philokalia* of Macarius of Corinth and Nicodemus the Hagiorite

It seems paradoxical that the eighteenth century, the period of the Enlightenment and the triumph of rationalism, was also that of a new renaissance of Athonite hesychasm. In the fourteenth and fifteenth centuries, the Jesus prayer had spread out from the Holy Mountain to the whole Orthodox world. After a period of decline, Athos again became a center for the diffusion of the theory and the practice of the Jesus prayer. We could even say that the survival of hesychasm on Mount Athos was essentially due to the fact that it was as a closed universe, isolated on the outer limits of Mediterranean Europe and cut off from modern western culture. As such, Mount Athos could not be penetrated by exterior influences, whether secular or religious. In reality, things were rather more complex. Subtle links united different worlds which, nonetheless, breathed the same cultural and intellectual air. The idea of gathering together all human knowledge in a vast encyclopedia was part of the atmosphere during the second half of the eighteenth century. It is, therefore, not unreasonable to think that this idea stood behind the project that produced the great collection of ascetical and mystical texts called the *Philokalia*[1] which was published in Venice in 1782. For centuries, Venice had been the main meeting point between East and West. While the *Philokalia* may seem quite similar in form to the *Encyclopedia*, its purpose was, in fact, the exact opposite. To the man of rational clarity, it opposed the hidden man of the heart – *homo cordis absconditus*; to the knowledge of the multifaceted exterior world – *partes extra partes* – it opposed the experience of those who had been "reduced to the essential," who were alert, the "neptics." These were men who longed for the uncreated Light of the incandescent Uni-Trinity and seemed to be drawn to it.

The *Philokalia* was both the fruit and the instrument by which the ancient mystical tradition of the Christian East was transmitted. The rediscovery of this tradition was carried out by men who not only knew the West in its many facets but who were particularly open to Western spiritual influences.

The word *Philokalia* means "love of beauty," and it must be understood as the love of spiritual beauty in the hellenic sense of the term which identified or associated the beautiful with the good.[2] The first Greek *Philokalia* was published anonymously even though we know who the compilers were: Metropolitan Macarius of Corinth (1731–1805) and Nicodemus of Naxos (1748–1809), called "the Hagiorite" because he lived on the Holy Mountain. Macarius was deposed from his diocese under pressure from the Turks and spent the rest of his life wandering from place to place. He stayed on Mount Athos several times and died as a hermit on Chios. Nicodemus was a talented writer and an exceptionally erudite man, both in literature and theology. He was the

---

[1] The full title is *Philokalia of the Holy Neptics Gathered Together from among the Holy God-bearing Fathers Wherein We See How, by the Philosophy of the Active Life and Contemplation, the Mind Is Purified, Illuminated, and Made Perfect.* The format of the work was a folio volume of 1207 double-columned pages. All the copies were taken back to the East.

[2] *Kalos k'agathos*, beautiful and good. The association of these two adjectives was characteristic of the æsthetical and ethical ideal of ancient Greece, an ideal taken up and creatively recast by Eastern monasticism.

author of various hagiographical, liturgical, and mystical works, and, not satisfied simply to collect classical texts on hesychasm, he also composed an original and personal treatise on hesychastic prayer.[3] He was canonized in 1955 on the initiative of the ecumenical patriarch Athenagoras I and the Holy Synod of Constantinople.

Both Macarius and Nicodemus were open to certain ideas of the Latin West. In his treatise *On the Participation in the Holy Mysteries,* Macarius showed himself to be in favor of frequent communion which at the time was considered a Latinizing practice. Nicodemus translated the work of an Italian monk, Lorenzo Scupoli, *The Spiritual Struggle,* and, even more surprisingly, he adapted Ignatius Loyola's *Spiritual Exercises* for Orthodox use.

Macarius' association of the Jesus prayer with a spirituality centered on the eucharistic mystery was a new and important development. He integrated the prayer of the "solitary ones" with the main liturgical and mystical stream at the heart of Orthodox ecclesial piety. This was important because the "solitary ones" at times appeared to drift away from that main stream. Liturgical prayer was thus spiritualized and interiorized; it lost the heaviness of ritualism that tended to lead to inertia. In return, the liturgy brought its own richness to hesychastic spirituality, thus preserving it from the hyper-spiritualized abstraction that had often been its temptation.

The *Philokalia* of Macarius and Nicodemus[4] is a collection of texts from different periods and origins that have been

---

[3] The work of St. Nicodemus the Hagiorite is called *The Handbook of Exhortations on Keeping Watch Over the Five Senses, the Imagination, the Mind and the Heart.* Fr. Hausherr has translated part of it into French in *Méthode de Prière Hésychaste* [Methods of Hesychastic Prayer], pp. 107 ff.

[4] Copies of Nicodemus and Macarius' first *Philokalia* are extremely rare. Reprints of the Greek *Philokalia* were made in Athens in 1893 and in 1956–63. A French translation by Jacques Touraille is underway and being published by Abbaye de Bellefontaine. In English, see *The Philokalia*, Faber and Faber, London, 1979.

carried along by the great river of Eastern monasticism. It is also a considerable work, a sort of "summum" on the Jesus prayer that has been translated into Church Slavonic,[5] Romanian, and modern Russian. In the nineteenth century, the *Philokalia* along with the Gospels were the spiritual viaticum of thousands of Orthodox Christians.

The *Starets* Paisius Velichkovsky and the Flourishing of Hesychasm in Moldavia and Russia

The name of the Ukrainian *starets*, Paisius Velichkovsky, is associated with the diffusion of the prayer of the heart and with the renewal of contemplative monasticism in Slavic and Moldavian regions.

Paisius' personal story is important for the history of the hesychastic movement in modern times.[6] He was born in 1722 at Poltava in Ukraine, that is, an "area near the border," according to the meaning of the word *Ukraine*, and was baptized with the name Peter. In his native region, the Orthodox East and the Latin West had for centuries met and clashed. At a very young age, Paisius was attracted to the monastic life. His favorite reading was the *Lives of the Saints*, and he dreamed of imitating the ascetical exploits of the *podvizhniki*.[7] Coming from a family of parish priests, he was expected to take his father's place when the latter died at an early age. When he was 14, Paisius nonetheless had to prepare himself for his future ministry and so entered Kiev's Græco-Latin academy on a scholarship. This school was the

---

[5] Slavonic is an archaic language that is used today only in the liturgy of the Russian, Serbian, and Bulgarian Churches.

[6] The *starets* Paisius was recently canonized at the local council of the Russian Orthodox Church in June, 1988. His biography was written, in Russian, by Fr. Sergius Tchetverikov, Petcheri, Estonia, 1938, and in French by I. Smolitsch, *Moines de la Sainte Russie* [Monks of Holy Russia], Paris, Editions Mame, 1967, pp. 80 ff. In English, see Sergius Bolshakoff, *Russian Mystics*, Cistercian Publications, Inc., Kalamazoo, Michigan, 1977, pp. 79–98.

[7] The *podviznik* is a "spiritual wrestler," an ascetic.

famous Orthodox Church school where studies were organized on the model of the Jesuit colleges in nearby Poland. Here the young schoolboy acquired an intellectual education and a knowledge of ancient languages that would later on allow him to become a translator. But at the time, the young seminarian, who had always dreamed of a return to the authentic tradition of the Fathers, was repulsed by the academic teaching whose scholasticism only disgusted him and left him spiritually hungry. He criticized the "academic" monks for being "puffed up with pride," perverted by a "pagan wisdom" that drew them away from the simplicity and the pure doctrine of the Gospel. He considered the Latinizing teaching of the academy to be pagan because it was based on the humanism of the Renaissance. The young man decided one evening to run away, like a thief in the night, and thus abandoned his studies which might have caused him to lose his soul.

For many years, all along the uncertain boundaries between the Ukraine, Poland, and Moldavia, Paisius led the life of a pilgrim-vagabond. He was in search of a place of prayer and more especially a "spiritual father in tune with his heart." According to the circumstances of the moment, Paisius wandered around from one monastery to another without settling anywhere in particular. In 1741, at the age of 19, he received the monastic tonsure with the name of Platon from an *elder* who sensed that he was authentically dedicated to prayer. His spiritual quest was nonetheless to continue, and in 1746 he arrived on Mount Athos where a new disappointment awaited him. Most of the monasteries on Athos were at that time in a state of deep spiritual decadence. No one seemed to be interested in the aspirations of the young monk, who went through years of great poverty and moral solitude on the Holy Mountain. Even though he did not have a "spiritual father" who could guide him on the path of contemplative prayer, he did eventually find "the treasure hidden in a field," according to the gospel parable. While he was digging around in monastery libraries, he came across the writings of a prestigious ancestor, the *starets* Nil Sorsky (1433–1508) who in the second half of the fifteenth century had been a promoter of hesychastic life in Muscovite Russia. For the young monk, Scripture reading and St Nil's work, itself a mosaic of patristic quotes, replaced the oral teaching that he had never received from his master. Following the advice of Nil and having changed his name from Platon to Paisius when he took on the great monastic schema, he opted for a middle road between the life of a hermit and community life as it was practiced in the large monasteries. He thus took up monastic life in a "skete," that is, a small fraternal group of monks. In a skete, all that is necessary is a simple and flexible rule that the "spiritual father" can adapt to the personality of each of his "children" by assessing each one's degree of maturity. Rather quickly, Paisius' reputation attracted other monks or novices who wanted to share his way of life. Against his will, it seems, a good sized community took shape. The quarters used at the beginning were now too small. Paisius and his monks finally left Athos and went to Moldavia, the home of several of his companions, where they were able to find protectors.

First at Dragomirna and then at Niamets, Fr. Paisius organized his community's life in accordance with the rules of St Basil the Great and Theodore the Studite while at the same time adding elements from the specifically hesychastic tradition. One such important element was the charismatic ministry of the spiritual father which he managed to establish despite institutional resistance. The community life of the monks was organized without rigidity, taking into account everyone's personal calling. The goal was to harmonize work, whether intellectual or manual, and prayer aiming at a balance between solitary prayer and collective singing of Psalms in church.

The *starets* received hundreds of visitors from various Orthodox regions but also from other European countries.

He wrote many letters, and his influence spread through his literary works which contain a treatise called *A Letter on the Monastic Life Addressed to the Adversaries and the Detractors of Spiritual Prayer*[8] and especially a Slavic translation of the *Philokalia* called *Dobrotolyubie*. This translation was edited and distributed in Russia through the support of Metropolitan Gabriel of St Petersburg who, even though he was a court prelate, a friend of Catherine II, and a reader of French philosophers, remained an authentic monk at heart and wanted to promote the renaissance of contemplative prayer.

The appearance of this Slavic version of the *Philokalia* was a historical event just as important as the publication of the original collection. The *Dobrotolyubie* of Paisius Velichkovsky circulated hand-to-hand and was treated as a precious treasure. The *Dobrotolyubie* fed the spiritual and charismatic element in the Russian Church, as did two other Russian translations which followed in its wake; we will deal with them later on. It was to this spirituality that the great Russian *startsi* of the nineteenth century adhered. St Seraphim of Sarov (1759–1833),[9] whose essentially pentecostal spirituality was to have such a great influence, was guided to the Sarov monastery by one of Paisius' disciples. In *The Instructions* of St Seraphim, we find the following lines on the Jesus prayer which indicate that he had a profound experience while using it in prayer:

> In order to receive and feel the light of Christ in your heart, you must, as much as possible, move away from all visible things. When the soul, filled with an interior faith in the crucified Lord, is purified by penitence and good works, you must close your physical eyes, let your understanding descend into your heart, and continuously call

---

[8] The periodical *Pout*, Paris, 1926–27, #3 and #7, in Russian. Extracts are found in Smolitsch, pp. 89 ff.

[9] On Seraphim of Sarov, besides the works already quoted, see in French, Irina Gorainoff, *Séraphin de Sarov* [Serpahim of Sarov], Bellefontaine, 1972 (republished by Desclée de Brouwer, collection Théophanie) and in English *Russian Mystics*, pp. 122–43.

out the name of our Lord Jesus Christ: "Lord Jesus Christ, Son of God, have mercy on me." Then, in relation to each person's zeal and the attachment of his spirit to the Beloved, he will find in the invocation of the Name delights that will awaken in him the will to seek out the highest illumination.[10]

In the middle of the nineteenth century, the famous Optino hermitage, described by Dostoevsky in *The Brothers Karamazov*, became a center for the spreading of the prayer of the heart.

It was not only to the monasteries that this spirituality brought life. Like an underground river, its influence could be felt in all the classes of Russian society. Thanks to the *Dobrotolyubie*, methods of contemplative prayer became familiar not only to a handful of monks but also to simple peasants, aristocrats, merchants and even westernized intellectuals of mid-nineteenth century Russia. *The Way of the Pilgrim*,[11] whose spiritual freshness has charmed thousands of Russian and Western readers, is a work that witnesses to the diffusion of the prayer of the heart among the Christian people.

The Way of the Pilgrim

The pilgrim (*strannik*) was a typical figure in ancient Russian society[12]; he was a poor lame peasant who traveled

---

[10] Translated into English from a French translation by A Monk of the Eastern Church, p. 57. Another slightly different French translation is found in Smolitsch, p. 213.

[11] The work appeared in 1884 in Kazan under the title *Sincere Tales of a Pilgrim to His Spiritual Father.* Another edition was published in 1911 by the St Sergius Monastery, Moscow. The origins of this anonymous work remain mysterious. Was it the exact transcription of an oral autobiographical account, or is it a literary work? There are several French translations of the first part; most available in the collection *Livre de Vie*, #63 by Jean Laloy. The second part has been published by Abbaye de Bellefontaine, 1973. In English, see *The Way of the Pilgrim and The Pilgrim Continues his Way*, Seabury, New York, 1965.

[12] See Michel Evdokimov, *Pèlerins russes et vagabonds mystiques* [Russian Pilgrims and Mystical Vagabonds], Editions du Cerf, Paris, 1987.

all over Russia and Siberia with a knapsack that contained dried bread and the Bible. He asked a *starets* about the way to practice the Apostle's advice, "Pray without ceasing." The *starets* then explained to him the practice of the Jesus prayer and had him read some passages of the *Dobrotolyubie*. He made the pilgrim submit to a progressively arduous training: first 3,000 invocations a day, then 6,000, and then 12,000. At a certain point, the pilgrim stopped counting the number of invocations because the prayer "Lord Jesus Christ, Son of God, have mercy on me a sinner" had aligned itself with each breath, with each heartbeat. Finally no words were spoken at all: "The lips stopped moving, and the only thing left to do was to listen to the heart speak."[13]

The pilgrim met many people, and whether it was a peasant, civil servant, or landowner, he was able to find a brother who shared his longing for ceaseless prayer. He also had terrifying adventures, was hungry, thirsty, and encountered dangers from both nature and men. The prayer was for him at such times a protection and a consolation.

> When the bitter cold cuts through me, I repeat my prayer with even more fervor, and I feel warmed up. When hunger begins to torture me, I invoke the name of Jesus Christ more often, and I forget that I want to eat. . . . If someone hurts me, I just think "how sweet is the Jesus prayer," and the offense and the resentment fly away and are forgotten. I have nearly lost all feeling; I have no cares; I have no desires; nothing attracts me. The only thing that I desire is to pray, pray without ceasing, and when I pray, I am filled with joy.[14]

The fruits of ceaseless prayer are, along with joy and tenderness of the heart, a feeling of "lightness and liberty," love for the whole of creation, an attitude that seems to be typical of Russian Christian spirituality.

---

[13] A Monk . . . p. 61.
[14] An English translation of a French text from *Récits d'un pèlerin, Irénikon,* Amay-sur-Meuse, 1928, pp. 13 ff.

Sometimes, there was such a bubbling up in my heart and a lightness, a freedom, a joy so great that I was transformed and felt in ecstasy. Sometimes I felt a burning love for Jesus Christ and for the whole divine creation. Sometimes, my tears flowed all on their own in thanksgiving to the Lord who had mercy on me, such a hardened sinner. Sometimes, my limited mind was illuminated. . . . Sometimes the sweet warmth of my heart spilled over into all my being, and I felt the presence of the Lord with great emotion. Sometimes, I felt a powerful and deep joy on invoking the name of Jesus Christ, and I understood the meaning of his saying, "The Kingdom of God is within you."

Everything, however, is not pure gold in this story. The prayer sometimes seems too mechanical, operating *ex opere operato,* for example, when a tyrannical master imposed it on a young servant . . .

The spiritual father disappeared from the story after giving a very quick initiation to the pilgrim who then educated himself. He was preserved from the illusions of his imagination by humility and simplicity of heart. The example of the pilgrim, if it were detached from its religious and cultural context, could not be followed to the letter without running certain risks. The image is, nonetheless, inspiring. *The Way of the Pilgrim* introduces its readers to a way of using the Jesus prayer that could be called "evangelical." As such, it is without complicated psychosomatic techniques and is carried along only by faith and love.

Modern Elaborations

Other masters of the Jesus prayer in the second half of the nineteenth century were educated on a model of theological reflection and introspection not at all like the spontaneity of the "pilgrim." They tried to define more clearly the stages of the spiritual quest by setting out the risks of delusion and mental wandering, dangers that stalk those who journey on the spiritual way. Two other translators of the *Philokalia* belong to this prudent but somewhat rigorist tendency. They were at the same time writers and attentive spiritual directors: Ignatius Brianchaninov (1807–1867) and Theophanes Govorov, known as the Recluse (1815–1894).[15]

Before becoming a monk, Ignatius had distinguished himself by his brilliant studies in a school of military engineering. Both were very well-versed in secular and theological matters. Both men were also bishops for several years, and retired from active life to devote themselves entirely to prayer and the direction of their spiritual children.

As a young monk, Ignatius accepted the direction of the *starets* Leonide, the first in the line of the famous Optino *startsi.* He made a Russian translation of the *Philokalia,* published in St Petersburg in 1857, and also wrote a treatise called *On the Jesus Prayer* as well as an autobiography. His letters were published after his death and reveal the attitude, austere but not without spiritual warmth, by which he guided his spiritual children.[16]

---

[15] These two great spiritual masters were recently canonized at the local council of the Russian Church, June, 1988.

[16] On Ignatius Brianchaninov in French, see Sr. Philareta Engelund, *Approches de la prière de Jésus, introduction biographique* [Approaches to the Jesus Prayer: A Biographical Introduction], Fr. Symeon, trans., Bellefontaine, 1983, and Ignatius Brianchaninov, *Traité sur la prière de Jésus* [Treatise on the Jesus Prayer], Fr. Symeon, trans., Bellefontaine. In English, see Ignatius Brianchaninov, *On the Prayer of Jesus,* Fr. Lazarus, trans., John M. Watkins, London, 1965, and *Russian Mystics*, pp. 144–165.

Bishop Theophanes was a former student of the ecclesiastical Academy of Kiev and an intellectual monk. He taught philosophy and then moral theology at Kiev, Novgorod, and finally at the ecclesiastical Academy of St Petersburg. During his stays in the East as a member of the Russian mission in Jerusalem, he came in contact with Palestinian monasticism. As bishop of Tambov and then Vladimir, he distinguished himself as a preacher thus following the example of St Tikhon of Zadonsk whom he admired very much. Bishop Theophanes was present at and actively participated in the canonization of St Tikhon, and like his illustrious predecessor, he affirmed that theological faith, when it is authentic, normally extends itself into personal and social ethics which it inspires and illuminates.

After seven years of pastoral activity, bishop Theophanes asked to be allowed to retire from the world. He was given the hermitage of Vychna where he lived for 28 years slowly burning himself up like "a candle before the face of God."[17]

Both Ignatius Brianchaninov and Theophanes Govorov knew, practiced, and propagated hesychastic prayer. The first translated into modern Russian passages of the *Philokalia* while the second produced a more complete translation in cooperation with the Russian monastery of St Panteleimon on Mount Athos.[18] Neither of them, however, was simply a transmitter. Both steeped themselves in the ancient tradition, decanting and purifying it. Through a theological reflection and rigorous spiritual requirements, they filtered out the tradition's impurities. Both men benefited from the renewal of patristic studies in the Russian ecclesiastical academies of

---

[17] Smolitsch, op. cit., p. 150. For bibliographies on Bishop Theophanes, see *ibid.*, p. 223, #70; and *Russian Mystics*, pp. 298–300. For a German translation of some of his letters, see "Briefe eines Starzen," van Bubnov, trans., *Russische Frömmigkeit*, Wiesbaden, 1947.

[18] The *Dobrotolyubie* of Ignatius Brianchaninov was published in St Petersburg, 1857, while the text of Theophanes was edited by St Panteleimon's monastery on Mt. Athos, 1877.

the nineteenth century as well as from the living tradition of the Jesus prayer based on Paisius' work. Like the spirituality of Tikhon of Zadonsk, that of Ignatius and Theophanes was marked by a certain Orthodox Augustinianism that was characterized by lucid introspection, a sense of sin, and an emphasis on grace as free and all-powerful.[19]

In line with this approach, Ignatius and Theophanes mistrusted "exterior methods" by which they meant psycho-somatic methods. These methods should be seen as crutches and are not important in themselves. They were "means" that must not be confused with the end result. Theophanes spoke of them as "exterior preparations for interior activity to which they added nothing essential."[20] To a legitimate prudence and a critical attitude toward all mechanical processes, we must no doubt add the influence of "spiritualist" or "paral-lelist" psychology of the nineteenth century. It was sometimes said that from then on, exterior processes should be omitted because "they scandalize some and put off others from practicing the prayer. For others they deform the exer-cise itself."[21]

Even if all quietism is to be rejected and the ascetical struggle recognized as necessary, it would nonetheless be pointless to see in asceticism anything other that a prepa-ration for receiving divine grace. Ascetical practices must not lead to pride but to an awareness of man's powerless-ness when abandoned to himself and to his weakness. Theophanes the Recluse wrote the following:

> To attach one's hope to any personal work, even if it is by one single hair, is already to turn away from the straight and narrow path. If you withdraw into solitude with the idea

---

[19] These two authors' teaching on the Jesus prayer is the basis of our study "La Prière de Jésus," *Dieu Vivant* #8, 1947, and re-edited in *Douloureuse Joie* [Painful Joy] Bellefontaine, 1974. In 1936, the Valamo monastery (Finland) published a Russian volume on the Jesus prayer which contains many pas-sages from the writings of Ignatius Brianchaninov and Theophanes Govorov.

[20] A Monk . . . p. 58.

[21] *Ibid.*

that by your prostrations, prayers, and nighttime vigils, everything will be changed, the Lord will purposefully not grant you the promised grace until all hope in your works has evaporated. This is true even though without your works, you cannot receive anything. . . . Work hard therefore until you are exhausted. Expend your energy til the last degree, but wait only on the Lord to bring about the work of salvation. . . . The Lord always desires what is for our salvation, and he is always ready to give it to us. He is simply waiting for us to be ready and capable of receiving his gifts. The question "How can I learn to keep watch over myself?" should rather be put this way, "How can I always be ready to receive salutary strength which is ever ready to come down on us from the Lord?" To open ourselves to grace is to "know that we are empty . . ." It is to know that the Lord alone can, wants, and knows how to fill that emptiness.[22]

Ignatius and Theophanes systematized the ascetical teaching of the Fathers and hardened somewhat the traditional distinctions. They discerned three degrees of prayer:

1. "laborious" prayer where the effort of the will predominates;
2. "spontaneous" or charismatic prayer (samodviznaia) which is the gift of grace; and
3. "contemplation" beyond all verbal prayer.

The essential element, even in the "active" phase of prayer, is not its quantity. Theophanes: "Do not worry about the number of prayers that you recite; your only care should be to let your prayer bubble up from your heart as from a spring of running water." At the beginning, laborious prayer may seem like going across the desert where each traveler must voluntarily close his eyes to all consoling mirages, to all imaginary representations.

The simplest rule about prayer is to let no images come into our mind, having concentrated our mind in the heart, to hold fast to the conviction that God is near, that he sees and hears, to bow down before him. . . . We must work at

---

[22] *Douloureuse Joie*, p. 98.

praying without images. Keep your mind in your heart and be confident that God is there, but do not try to picture to yourself what he is like.[23]

True attention in prayer is simply waiting in faith.

Ignatius and Theophanes' "sobriety" and their mistrust of the imagination seem to go against the emotional spontaneity of the pilgrim who in his thoughts "threw himself at Christ's feet . . . holding him in his embrace and tenderly kissing his feet." In the Jesus prayer, as in the Father's house, there are no doubt many mansions. In any case, we must remember that Ignatius was writing especially to monks and nuns who were certainly more tempted than a simple peasant to let themselves be carried away by their imaginations and to fall into pride about so-called "mystical graces." For these monastics, renunciation of the imagination can be a guard-rail, but it can also lead to a certain spiritual dryness when it is built up into a system. The Lord who became totally human also assumed the power of the imagination which is part of that humanity. He did this so that he could purify the imagination and make it fruitful by grace. It would thus cease to be "the mistress of error and falsehood" and would become an "instrument of glorification and thanksgiving."

Ignatius Brianchaninov wanted above all to avoid interpreting the Jesus prayer as a kind of self-control technique, or as we might say today, a stress management therapy. He thus very clearly distinguished between the work of our will and the work of divine grace. Laborious prayer, he writes, is comparable to the floor of the sanctuary or the porticoes of the pool of Bethesda where the sick gathered while waiting for the angel to stir up the water and heal them. "But the Lord himself, and only he, in his own good time, will grant healing and entry into the sanctuary according to his ineffable and incomprehensible benevolence."[24]

---

[23] *Ibid.*, p. 110.
[24] *Ibid.*, p. 111.

In line with the traditional teaching of the Eastern spiritual masters, this healing is seen essentially as a reunification in Christ of man's divided self which sin had shattered:

> Having prepared the vase, all of a sudden and in an immaterial and unexpected way, [grace] touches the separated parts, and they all come together. Who did the touching? I cannot explain it. I saw nothing, heard nothing, but I feel changed. . . . The Creator acts to bring about a "restoration" as he acted to bring about the creation. When his hands touched my being, my intelligence, my heart, and my body came together to constitute a complete whole. They were then plunged into God and remain there as long as the invisible, ungraspable, and all-powerful Hand sustains them.[25]

Theophanes rejected the misunderstandings created by naively realistic and objectivizing descriptions of mystical experience and tried to suggest what it was in essence: "The essence of practicing the Jesus prayer is to acquire the habit of staying, by the intelligence, in the heart which feels the presence of God but not physically."[26] This is a formula worthy of being studied.

For those who have practiced the method of hesychastic prayer, "this calm and slow descent of the intelligence into the heart" corresponds to a very real experience even though it is unspeakable and "would be pointless to want to describe on paper."[27]

The concise and purposefully simple form that Theophanes the Recluse used to express this experience is characteristic of a distillation and a focusing which took place on Mt Athos where his version of the *Dobrotolyubie* was published.

As we reach the end of this rapid historical study of the hesychastic Tradition, we will conclude with some brief **comments about the Jesus prayer in our time.**

---

[25] *Ibid.*, p. 113.
[26] A Monk . . .., pp. 58–59.
[27] *Ibid.*, p. 115.

CHAPTER NINE

The Jesus Prayer in the West Today

The invocation of Jesus' name is in no way foreign to western Christian spirituality. The Roman missal contains a feast of the Holy Name of Jesus as an expression of a widespread devotion of the late Middle Ages, especially popular in Franciscan circles. Saint Bernard of Sienna (1380–1444) was the great preacher of this devotion. Beginning in the twelfth century, St Bernard of Clairvaux developed a theology and spirituality of Jesus' name in some of his sermons, for example sermon 15 on the Song of Songs.[1]

The veneration of Jesus' name, therefore, has deep and ancient roots in Western, as well as in Eastern, Christian piety.[2]

However, it is only rather recently that the West has become interested in the Jesus prayer as a specific technique and method of prayer. The Jesus prayer was for a long time denounced by the Latin adversaries of Gregory Palamas and ridiculed by theologians. The average Christian in the West knew nothing about it.

---

[1] PL, t. 183.
[2] Those who are interested in this problem can consult Appendix II of the work we have often quoted by A Monk of the Eastern Church.

The Jesus Prayer in the Russian Emigration

The Russian emigration of the twentieth century has played an unquestionably important role in the diffusion of the Jesus prayer in the West. In the period between the First and the Second World Wars, this group of exiles provided the milieu for a veritable renaissance of the Jesus prayer, both in relation to the practice of the prayer and the publication of source material and theoretical reflection.

On the level of practice, this renaissance was characterized by a diffusion of the prayer of the heart among laypeople, a phenomenon that had already begun in Russia. The Bolshevik Revolution eliminated the monastic centers and dispersed the monks. In very difficult, often desperate, material conditions, the Russian diaspora tried to preserve the essential spiritual treasures of Orthodoxy. For many men and women who formerly belonged to the privileged classes of Russia and who were forced to earn their living working in mines, factories or the fields, the invocation of Jesus' name was the only prayer they could manage: a very simple invocation, without any special technique but compatible with the crushing monotony of certain kinds of work. The Jesus prayer allowed these workers to endure such work, and even transfigured it.

Nadejda Gorodetzky who lived through those times asked, "Is it a monk's prayer?" She answered her own question in this way: "The Jesus prayer was indeed widely practiced by the lay people of the Orthodox Church. It is so simple that it is not necessary to learn it to remember it. . . . Many went about their habitual work repeating this prayer."[3]

---

[3] N. Godoretsky, "The Prayer of Jesus," *Blackfriars*, Feb., 1942. From the same milieu, Paul Fidler, a Franco-Russian author and eternal God-seeker, *L'Homme est prière* [Man is Prayer], Paris, 1951.

In 1928, a new Russian edition of the *Philokalia* was published in Harbin, Manchuria, where a sizable Russian colony had taken up residence. During the same period in Paris, a Russian religious thinker, B. Vycheslavtsev, reprinted the first part of the *Way of the Pilgrim*. The Valamo monastery in Finland was one of the rare Russian monasteries that survived the Revolution, and it became a center for the diffusion of the Jesus prayer. Many works on the subject were also written there.[4]

Still during the inter-war period, Fr. Sergius Bulgakov worked out a "philosophy of the name," which in his mind was intimately tied to the Jesus prayer. Fr. Sergius was a professor at St Sergius Orthodox Theological Institute in Paris, a center dedicated to perpetuating the theological tradition of the Russian Church. In his work *The Orthodox Church*[5], he affirmed that the "theological doctrine of God's name is a problem essential to the expression of Orthodoxy."

We must include the name of Fr. Tchetverikov among those who made known the Jesus prayer. He was one of the leaders and main inspirations of the Russian Christian Students' Movement. He also wrote an important work on Paisius Velichkovsky.[6]

The Jesus Prayer in Western Religious Literature

The interest that Western Christians have shown for the Jesus prayer is but an extension of a meeting with living

---

[4] Before the Second World War, Valamo published a *Recueil sur la prière de Jé-sus* [Collection of Works on the Jesus Prayer] in two volumes, which, among other things, contained texts by Paisius Velichkovsky, Ignatius Brianchani-nov, and Theophane the Recluse.

[5] Paris, 1932, p. 208, in French. Bulgakov devoted an important work to the "philosophy of the name," Eilosofiya imeni, Paris, 1953, in Russian. See An-toine Nivière, "Les moines onomatodores et l'intelligentsia russe" [The Name-Carrying Monks and the Russian Intelligentsia], *Cahiers du monde russe et soviétique*, 1988.

[6] Paris, 1938, in Russian.

Orthodoxy, a meeting that was made possible by the Russian diaspora. After the two world wars, various intellectual currents found themselves on the same wave length with the longing for spiritual renewal: renewal of patristic studies, the ecumenical movement, an interest in "Eastern" philosophies and wisdoms, a rediscovery of the psychosomatic complex by medicine and psychoanalysis.

In 1927, the scholarly work of Fr. Irénée Hausherr opened the path to studies by Byzantine scholars on the method of hesychastic prayer.[7]

Other publications were produced by ecumenical circles. In 1928, the priory of Amay-sur-Meuse, dedicated as it was to Church union, published the first French translation of *The Way of the Pilgrim* in its revue *Irenikon*. There had already been a German translation and two English translations appeared in 1930.[8]

A new French translation of the *Pilgrim* by J. Gauvain, whose pseudonym was Jean Laloy, was published during the Second World War in 1943 in *Les Cahiers du Rhône* and republished in the collection "Livre de Vie" in Paris, 1966. It is impossible to enumerate all the other translations and re-publications of the *Pilgrim* that have appeared in nearly every Western language. How can we explain the unforeseen success of a work that, though it is moving, appeared to be destined for a limited circle of people who had specific cultural interests? In our time of so-called unbelief, the extent of the work's success certainly constitutes a puzzling spiritual phenomenon.

---

[7] I. Hausherr, "La Méthode d'oraison hésychaste" [The Method of Hesychastic Prayer], *Orientalia Christiania* IX, 2, 1927.

[8] a) *Ein russisches Pilgerleben*, Berlin, 1926; b) *The Story of a Russian Pilgrim*, Dom Theodor Bailey, trans., London, 1930; c) *The Way of the Pilgrim*, R. M. French, trans., London 1930.

As the pilgrim pursued his travels, the number of historical, psychological, and theological studies on hesychasm continued to grow.[9] These studies dealt especially with the psychosomatic methods that undergird the prayer of the heart, techniques that are sometimes associated with Eastern yoga, sometimes with a stress management or relaxation therapy invented by a Berlin doctor. A bibliography of such works would contain dozens even hundred of titles; here are two examples by Orthodox authors: Metropolitan (then priest-monk) Antony Bloom, *Hésychasme: yoga chrétien* [Hesychasm: Christian Yoga][10] and Dr. Paul Zacharias, *Prière et relaxation* [11]

In this vast literature, containing both weeds and good grain, there is a small book that we have often quoted by A Monk of the Eastern Church. Its quality lies in its clarity, synthetic character, and scholarship which devotes itself to spiritual *praxis*. Along with the *Petite Philocalie de la prière du cœur*, translated and presented by J. Gouillard, this book is no doubt the best and most accessible introduction to the Jesus prayer that is available to French speakers.[12] Those studies by Bishop Kallistos Ware, translated from English, should also be added to the list.

The success of these works proves that the interest in the Jesus prayer and hesychastic spirituality goes far beyond

---

[9] We are not going to deal with the important literature on Palamism.

[10] Hieromonk Anthony Bloom. "Hésychasme: Yoga chrétien," *Cahiers du Sud*, 1953, pp. 177–195. By the same author, though signed André Bloom, "Contemplation et Ascèse: contribution orthodoxe." *Etudes Carmélitaines 28*, Bruges, 1949. See also Gabriel Bornand. "Inde et christianisme: La méditation et la prière dans la tradition hésychaste et ses points de contact avec les traditions orientales," *Cahiers de St. Irénée*.

[11] "Gebet und Entspannung. Hesychastische Mystik und autogenes Training," *Die Welt zur Seele*, Gottingen, 1952. For an interesting bibliography on the Jesus prayer up to 1960, see A. Zigmund-Cerbu, "Lumières nouvelles sur le yoga et l'hésychasme," *Contacts 87*, 1973/3.

[12] Various studies on the prayer of the heart have been published in "Spiritualité orientale" of the Cistercian Abbey of Bellefontaine: among others, see Jacques Serr and Olivier Clement, *La Prière du Cœur*.

the borders of Orthodoxy and is by no means limited to monastic or Byzantinist circles.

This diffusion is not simply of theoretical interest It also concerns the use, the practice of the Jesus prayer. Even though it continues to be practiced in a traditional setting in Greece and on Mount Athos where it is undergoing a renaissance, the prayer of the heart is not limited to Western Orthodox monks but many others are also using it: Catholic Cistercians, Anglican nuns, and anonymous lay people.

The geographical and cultural extent of the diffusion of the Jesus prayer today is a new phenomenon, and it brings with it certain problems: Are there not risks, even serious dangers, in the fact that men and women, sometimes living in the world, sometimes not even Orthodox, have adopted a practice that was worked out by and for Eastern Orthodox monks? Similar questions may be asked concerning the association of the methods used in the Jesus prayer and those used in yoga and stress management therapy. Though we do not claim to have any definitive answers, we would like to formulate certain remarks in the hope of stimulating some reflective thinking.

Use and Misuse of the Jesus Prayer

Nothing in Orthodox doctrine makes a monk into a sort of "initiated master" of Eastern gnostic teachings, a guru whose task it is to reveal to lay people spiritual secrets to which only he and other "masters" have access. Is not a monk a layman too, albeit one with a particular vocation? The very opposite is the case: a constant monastic tradition sends a monk guilty of spiritual pride to visit some simple believer who lives in the world in faith, hope and love. It is from this simple believer that the monk must discover the "secret of the king." The opposite can also happen, and we have seen how St Seraphim of Sarov brought Motovilov, a layman living in the world, into his luminous visions. We are in no way denying the specificity of the monastic way, essentially oriented as it is toward prayer. The monk is consecrated to and for just that. However, monks and laymen living in the world belong to the same people (*laos*) of God. The "angelic" vocation of the monk is also a vocation of service for this people and for all humanity called to be united in Christ in one single body. This vocation is accomplished by intercession, but may it not also take other forms? For example, showing the people of today who live in the desert of an inhuman world and who are thirsty for living water, the deep well dug by the spiritual labors of monks during more than 1000 years and sharing with such people its cool, fresh water. Is this not a contemporary form of monastic service, a way for monks to participate in the salvation of the world?

As for laymen who in our times practice the Jesus prayer, three dangers need to be avoided, even though they are dangers for monks as well:

1. dilettantism,
2. formalistic use of techniques, and
3. an alienating escapism into pseudo- or impersonal mysticism.

The call to practice the Jesus prayer is a serious matter that requires an equally serious commitment. To play games with the Jesus prayer on the level of a fad or superficial fashion can only lead to perversion. For a believer, Jesus' name is sacred. The commandment not to use the Lord's name in vain must guide our approach to this form of prayer. It would be sacrilegious to try out the Jesus prayer like trying a "joint" or going to a new kind of relaxation therapy "to get back in shape." The merciful Lord, however, knows how to discern the grain of faith, hope and love that such "experimentation" sometimes hides; he can use it to open a door to the sinner's heart. We must not forget that "we do not choose the Jesus prayer. We are called and led to it by God, if he judges it proper. We must devote ourselves to it by obedience to a vocation . . . in so far as other obediences do not have priority."[13]

This call and devotion can have several degrees. For some, the invocation of Jesus' name will be perhaps a particularly important episode on their spiritual journey. For others, the prayer will be one of their habitual forms of prayer. For still others, it will become *the* method around which their whole inner prayer life will revolve.

Between a dangerous and sacrilegious dilettantism and a total devotion to the Jesus prayer, which would seem to require a solitary life, there appears to be a middle way, a royal way for some. For someone engaged in an active life with many obligations that cannot be neglected, a short, but deep and conscious invocation of Jesus' name can be the spring to which he frequently returns for refreshment in the middle of the desert. It is a spring that never stops flowing in him, silently, rejuvenating him even when he no longer pronounces the words of the prayer.

Questions of method, rhythmic breathing, and physical position must be given their due in their proper place, which is secondary. The method can be a help; the interest of certain concentration techniques cannot be denied. Seen from the spiritual point of view, however, these techniques are neutral in themselves though useful in certain cases and at certain times. They can nonetheless become an obstacle to an authentic meeting with God, to the extent that they block the inner horizon. The essential element is not in the method but rather in the spirit in which the Jesus prayer is practiced.

A prayer which is technically perfect but which only facilitates personal development, spiritual power and enjoyment, and psychic superiority is by its very nature a bad prayer. A humble prayer, spoken with faith, even if in an apparent state of spiritual dryness, whatever one's physical position,

---

[13] A Monk . . . p. 73.

will certainly be pleasing to the Lord. This is true for the Jesus prayer as well as for all other prayers.

The Jesus prayer is a way of uniting ourselves with Christ in the Spirit, by pronouncing Jesus' name as the carrier of the energies of the divine Word. It is a simple way but cannot be bypassed without ascetical effort and spiritual combat. It is a way of silence adapted to the needs of modern man who is saturated with noise and "bla-bla-bla"; it is a crucifying way for us who are so dispersed and whose sin is legion. We must be careful, however, not to go overboard with untimely propaganda and unenlightened zeal that claims that the Jesus prayer is "the best prayer" or the only one "that is right for our time."

There is a more subtle danger that would turn the Jesus prayer into a refuge, an enclosed garden of egocentric, private and non-ecclesial piety. This would be a serious misuse that would explain, and to a degree justify, the accusation that the interior life is a sort of opium, if not for the masses, at least for a protected elite.

But the Jesus prayer can also become a way of penetrating more deeply into the mystery of salvation that the Church has to announce to the world. If we meditate on the meaning of each word rather than repeating the words mechanically, we can open ourselves up to this mystery which becomes part of us in the communion of saints. "By pronouncing the name . . . we offer our flesh to the Word so that He takes it on himself in his mystical Body; we make the inner reality and the form of the word Jesus overflow into all our bodily members."[14] In the Jesus prayer, we are not looking for an escape route leading away from the cares of the world. We must deposit these cares at the Lord's feet in order to pick them back up with Him and in Him in a new way. A Monk of the Eastern Church has written that Jesus' name is an instrument, a transfiguring method that we can

---

[14] *Ibid.*, p. 78.

apply to the inanimate world, to the whole creation that is trying with every groan to move toward Christ, but especially to those persons whom God puts on our path:

> Jesus' name is a concrete and powerful way of transfiguring men in their deepest and most divine reality. The men and women we meet in the street, factory, office, and especially those who seem to be irritating and unlikable, let us go toward them with Jesus' name in our heart and on our lips. . . . If we see Jesus in each man, if we say "Jesus" over each person, we will go through the world with a new vision and with a new gift of our own heart. We can thus transform the world, as much as it is within us, and make our own the word Jacob spoke to his brother: "I saw your face and it was like seeing God's face." (Gn. 33:10)[15]

We earlier referred to the problem of the use of the Jesus prayer by men and women who are strangers to the cultural and spiritual context in which this practice was developed and took form. This is a real problem, but we need to make some distinctions and keep away from oversimplifications.

It would be historically untrue and spiritually sterile to see the Jesus prayer as the finished product, the crystallization of a culture and of a so-called monolithic "Eastern" spirituality. Our historical survey of the Jesus prayer has shown it to be "a movement" that has adapted itself with flexibility to diverse mentalities developing within spiritualities which, despite their profound unity, still allow variations: the rough spirituality of the desert, Mount Sinai's tenderness, the Greek intellectualism of Gregory Palamas, the simple, popular, and evangelical piety of the Russian Pilgrim. We must distinguish between the "spiritual" and the "cultural," even though these interpenetrate each other, and admit that the Spirit speaks different languages. The Jesus prayer has been assimilated and integrated by "Western" minds – the meaning of this word needs to be made clearer – and it has taken on a new face, and this is no bad thing. The work of A

---

[15] *Ibid.*, pp. 80–81.

Monk of the Eastern Church, so Western in some respects, appears to be the result of one of these creative integrations. Others are possible.

We must, however, be very aware of the danger of syncretism. The fact that Christians of other confessions practice the Jesus prayer cannot be interpreted in the Guenonian perspective of "the transcendental unity of religions." The use of the Jesus prayer outside the confession of Peter's faith appears to us to be always inconsistent and suspect, regardless of the personal sincerity of those who practice it. It is insufficient to see Jesus only as an avatar of the impersonal Divine or the interior image of "self."

The Jesus prayer is based on the faith of the *Una Sancta* and opens us to the mystery of the Body of Christ. It appears, therefore, as a way toward Christian unity. Whoever says this prayer and adheres profoundly to the divino-human person of Jesus – whatever may be the deficiencies in the expression of his faith – is potentially and invisibly in the Church. By pronouncing Jesus' name in a spirit of unconditional submission, we join Mary, the archetype of the Church, when the angel announced to her that she was to give birth to a son whose name would be "God saves."

A semantic analysis allows us to set out all the richness of meaning contained in the apparently so simple invocation of Jesus' name. Nonetheless, beyond all words and analysis, we must learn how to open ourselves to that which the words and analysis support: the living presence of Jesus. The goal of the Jesus prayer, which is also the fabric that must hold it together at every moment, is a living and ineffable contact with Christ and not a dissolution into an impersonal ocean. It is rather a suprapersonal meeting, an abyss of communion with the supreme Lover who is also the supreme Loved One and who introduces us into the loving kingdom of the Holy Trinity.

MEDITATION

The Power of the Name
The Jesus Prayer in Orthodox Spirituality

Bishop Kallistos of Diokleia

The Power of the Name

Prayer and Silence

"When you pray," it has been wisely said by an Orthodox writer in Finland, "you yourself must be silent.. . . . You yourself must be silent; let the prayer speak."[1] To achieve silence: this is of all things the hardest and the most decisive in the art of prayer. Silence is not merely negative a pause between words, a temporary cessation of speech – but, properly understood, it is highly positive: an attitude of attentive alertness, of vigilance, and above all of *listening*. The hesychast, the person who has attained *hesychia*, inner stillness or silence, is *par excellence* the one who listens. He listens to the voice of prayer in his own heart, and he understands that this voice is not his own but that of Another speaking within him.

The relationship between praying and keeping silent will become clearer if we consider four short definitions. The first is from *The Concise Oxford Dictionary*, which describes prayer as ". . . solemn request to God . . . formula used in praying". Prayer is here envisaged as something expressed in words, and more specifically as an act of asking God to confer some benefit. We are still on the level of external rather than inner prayer. Few of us can rest satisfied with such a definition.

Our second definition, from a Russian *starets* of the last century, is far less exterior. In prayer, says Bishop Theophane the Recluse (1815–94), "the principal thing is to stand before God with the mind in the heart, and to go on

---

[1] Tito Colliander, *The Way of the Ascetics*, London, 1960, p. 79.

standing before Him unceasingly day and night, until the end of life."[2] Praying, defined in this way, is no longer merely to ask for things, and can indeed exist without the employment of any words at all. It is not so much a momentary activity as a continuous state. To pray is to *stand before God*, to enter into an immediate and personal relationship with him; it is to know at every level of our being, from the instinctive to the intellectual, from the sub- to the supra-conscious, that we are in God and he is in us. To affirm and deepen our personal relationships with other human beings, it is not necessary to be continually presenting requests or using words; the better we come to know and love one another, the less need there is to express our mutual attitude verbally. It is the same in our personal relationship with God.

In these first two definitions, stress is laid primarily on what is done by the human person rather than by God. But in the relationship of prayer, it is the divine partner and not the human who takes the initiative and whose action is fundamental. This is brought out in our third definition, taken from St Gregory of Sinai (†1346). In an elaborate passage, where he loads one epithet upon another in his effort to describe the true reality of inner prayer, he ends suddenly with unexpected simplicity: "Why speak at length? Prayer is God, who works all things in all men."[3] *Prayer is God* – it is not something that I initiate but something in which I share; it is not primarily something that *I* do but something that *God* is doing in me: in St Paul's phrase, "not I, but Christ in me" (Gal 2:20). The path of inner prayer is exactly indicated in St John the Baptist's words about the Messiah: "He must increase, but I must decrease" (Jn 3:30). It is in this sense that to pray is to be silent. "You yourself

---

[2] Cited in Igumen Chariton of Valamo, *The Art of Prayer: An Orthodox Anthology*, trans. by E. Kadloubovsky and E. M. Palmer, London, 1966, p. 63.
[3] *Chapters*, 113, PG 150, 1280A. See Kallistos Ware, "The Jesus Prayer in St Gregory of Sinai," *Eastern Churches Review* iv, 1972, p. 8.

must be silent; let the prayer speak" – more precisely, let God speak. True inner prayer is to stop talking and to listen to the wordless voice of God within our heart; it is to cease doing things on our own, and to enter into the action of God. At the beginning of the Byzantine Liturgy, when the preliminary preparations are completed and all is now ready for the start of the Eucharist itself, the deacon approaches the priest and says: "It is time for the Lord to act."[4] Such exactly is the attitude of the worshipper not only at the Eucharistic Liturgy but in all prayer, public or private.

Our fourth definition, taken once more from St Gregory of Sinai, indicates more definitely the character of this action of the Lord within us. "Prayer," he says, "is the manifestation of Baptism."[5] The action of the Lord is not, of course, limited solely to the baptized; God is present and at work within all human kind, by virtue of the fact that each is created according to his divine image. But this image has been obscured and clouded over, although not totally obliterated, by our fall into sin. It is restored to its primal beauty and splendor through the sacrament of Baptism, whereby Christ and the Holy Spirit come to dwell in what the Fathers call "the innermost and secret sanctuary of our heart." For the overwhelming majority, however, Baptism is something received in infancy, of which they have no conscious memory. Although the baptismal Christ and the indwelling Paraclete never cease for one moment to work within us, most of us – save on rare occasions – remain virtually unaware of this inner presence and activity. The prayer,

---

[4] A quotation from Psalm 118 [119]-126. In some English versions of the Liturgy this is translated, "It is time to do [sacrifice] unto the Lord," but the alternative rendering which we have used is richer in meaning and is preferred by many Orthodox commentators.

The original Greek uses the word *kairos*: "It is the *kairos* for the Lord to act." *Kairos* bears here the special meaning of the decisive moment, the moment of opportunity: he who prays seizes the *kairos*. This is a point to which we shall return.

[5] *Chapters*, 113, PG 150, 1277D.

then, signifies the rediscovery and "manifestation, of baptismal grace. To pray is to pass from the state where grace is present in our hearts secretly and unconsciously, to the point of full inner perception and conscious awareness when we experience and *feel* the activity of the Spirit directly and immediately. In the words of St Kallistos and St Ignatios Xanthopoulos (fourteenth century), "The aim of the Christian life is to return to the perfect grace of the Holy and Life-giving Spirit,,which was conferred upon us at the beginning in divine Baptism."[6]

"In my beginning is my end." The purpose of prayer can be summarized in the phrase, "Become what you are." Become, consciously and actively, what you already are potentially and secretly, by virtue of your creation according to the divine image and your re-creation at Baptism. Become what you are: more exactly, return into yourself; discover him who is yours already, listen to him who never ceases to speak within you; possess him who even now possesses you. Such is God's message to anyone who wants to pray: "You would not seek me unless you had already found me."

But how are we to start? How, after entering our room and closing the door, are we to begin to pray, not just by repeating words from books, but by offering inner prayer, the living prayer of creative stillness? How can we learn to stop talking and to start listening:, Instead of simply speaking to God, how can we make our own the prayer in which God speaks to us? How shall we pass from prayer expressed in words to prayer of silence, from "strenuous" to "self acting" prayer (to use Bishop Theophane's terminology), from "my" prayer to the prayer of *Christ in me*?

One way to embark on this journey inwards is through the Invocation of the Name.

---

[6] *Century*, 4, PG 147, 637D. The idea of prayer as the discovery of God's ind-welling presence can be expounded equally in terms the Eucharist

"Lord Jesus . . ."

It is not, of course, the only way. No authentic relationship between persons can exist without mutual freedom and spontaneity, and this is true in particular of inner prayer. There are no fixed and unvarying rules, necessarily imposed on all who seek to pray; and equally there is no mechanical technique, whether physical or mental, which can compel God to manifest his presence. His grace is conferred always as a free gift, and cannot be gained automatically by any method or technique. The encounter between God and man in the kingdom of the heart is therefore marked by an inexhaustible variety of patterns, There are spiritual masters in the Orthodox Church who say little or nothing about the Jesus Prayer.[7] But, even if it enjoys no exclusive monopoly in the field of inner prayer, the Jesus Prayer has become for innumerable Eastern Christians over the centuries the standard path, the royal highway. And not for Eastern Christians only:[8] in the meeting between Orthodoxy and the West which has occurred over the past seventy years, probably no element in the Orthodox heritage has aroused such intense interest as the Jesus Prayer, and no single book has exercised a wider appeal than *The Way of a Pilgrim*. This enigmatic work, virtually unknown in pre-revolutionary Russia, has had a startling success in the non Orthodox world and since the 1920s has appeared in a

---

[7] The Jesus Prayer is nowhere mentioned, for example, in the authentic writings of St Symeon the New Theologian or in the vast spiritual anthology of Evergetinos (both of the eleventh century).

[8] There existed, of course, a warm devotion to the Holy Name of Jesus in the medieval West, not least in England. While this displays certain points of difference from the Byzantine tradition of the Jesus Prayer, there are also obvious parallels. See Kallistos Ware, "The Holy Name of Jesus in East and West: the Hesychasts and Richard Rolle," *Sobornost* 4:2, 1982, pp. 163–84.

wide range of languages.[9] Readers of J. D. Salinger will recall the impact of the "small pea-green cloth-bound book"[10] on Franny. Wherein, we ask, lies the distinctive appeal and effectiveness of the Jesus Prayer? Perhaps in four things above all: first, in its simplicity and flexibility; secondly, in its completeness; thirdly, in the power of the Name; and fourthly, in the spiritual discipline of persistent repetition. Let us take these points in order.

Simplicity and Flexibility

The Invocation of the Name is a prayer of the utmost simplicity, accessible to every Christian, but it leads at the same time to the deepest mysteries of contemplation. Anyone proposing to say the Jesus Prayer for lengthy periods of time each day – and, still more, anyone intending to use the breathing control and other physical exercises in conjunction with the Prayer – undoubtedly stands in need of a *starets*, of an experienced spiritual guide. Such guides are extremely rare in our day. But those who have no personal contact with a *starets* may still practise the Prayer without any fear, so long as they do so only for limited periods – initially, for no more than ten or fifteen minutes at a time – and so long as they make no attempt to interfere with the body's natural rhythms.

No specialized knowledge or training is required before commencing the Jesus Prayer. To the beginner it is sufficient to say: Simply begin. "In order to walk one must take a first step; in order to swim one must throw oneself into the water. It is the same with the Invocation of the Name. Begin to pronounce it with adoration and love. Cling

---

[9] It has even been translated into one of the major languages of the Indian sub-continent, Mahratti. The introduction to this translation has been written by a Hindu university professor who is a specialist in the spirituality of the Name: see E. R. Hambye SJ, in *Eastern Churches Review* v, 1973, p. 77.

[10] J. D. Salinger, *Franny and Zooey*.

to it. Repeat it. Do not think that you are invoking the Name; think only of Jesus himself. Say his Name slowly, softly and quietly."[11]

The outward form of the prayer is easily learnt. Basically it consists of the words "Lord Jesus Christ, Son of God, have mercy on me." There is, however, no strict uniformity. We can say ". . . have mercy on us," instead of "on me." The verbal formula can be shortened: "Lord Jesus Christ, have mercy on me," or "Lord Jesus," or even "Jesus" alone, although this last is less common. Alternatively, the form of words may be expanded by adding "a sinner" at the end, thus underlining the penitential aspect. We can say, recalling Peter's confession on the road to Caesarea Philippi, ". . . Son of the living God. . . . " Sometimes an invocation of the Mother of God or the saints is inserted. The one essential and unvarying element is the inclusion of the divine Name "Jesus." Each is free to discover through personal experience the particular form of words which answers most closely to his or her needs. The precise formula employed can of course be varied from time to time, so long as this is not done too often: for, as St Gregory of Sinai warns, "Trees which are repeatedly transplanted do not grow roots."[12]

There is a similar flexibility as regards the outward circumstances in which the Prayer is recited. Two ways of using the Prayer can be distinguished, the "free" and the "formal." By the "free" use is meant the recitation of the Prayer as we are engaged in our usual activities throughout the day. It may be said, once or many times, in the scattered moments which otherwise would be spiritually wasted: when occupied with some familiar and semi-automatic task, such as dressing, washing up, mending socks, or digging in the garden; when walking or driving, when waiting in a bus

---

[11] A Monk of the Eastern Church [Lev Gillet], *On the Invocation of the Name of Jesus*, The Fellowship of St Alban and St Sergius, London, 1950, pp. 5–6.
[12] *On stillness and the two ways of prayer*, 2, PG 1 50, 1316B.

queue or a traffic jam; in a moment of quiet before some especially painful or difficult interview; when unable to sleep, or before we have gained full consciousness on waking. Part of the distinctive value of the Jesus Prayer lies precisely in the fact that, because of its radical simplicity, it can be prayed in conditions of distraction when more complex forms of prayer are impossible. It is especially helpful in moments of tension and grave anxiety.

This "free" use of the Jesus Prayer enables us to bridge the gap between our explicit "times of prayer" – whether at church services or alone in our own room – and the normal activities of daily life "Pray without ceasing," St Paul insists (I Thess. 5:17): but how is this possible, since we have many other things to do as well? Bishop Theophane indicates the method in his maxim, "The hands at work, the mind and heart with God."[13] The Jesus Prayer, be coming by frequent repetition almost habitual and unconscious, helps us to stand in the presence of God wherever we are – not only in the sanctuary or in solitude, but in the kitchen, on the factory floor, in the office. So we become like Brother Lawrence, who "was more united with God during his ordinary activities than in religious exercises." "It is a great delusion," he remarked, "to imagine that prayer-time should be different from any other" for we are equally bound to be united to God by work at work-time as by prayer at prayer-time."[14]

The "free" recitation of the Jesus Prayer is complemented and strengthened by the "formal" use. In this second case we concentrate our whole attention on the saying of the Prayer, to the exclusion of all external activity. The Invocation forms part of the specific "prayer time" that we set aside for God each day. Normally, along with the Jesus Prayer, we shall also use in our "set" time other forms of prayer taken from

[13] *The Art of Prayer*. p. 92.
[14] Brother Lawrence of the Resurrection, (1611–91), Barefooted Carmelite, *The Practice of the Presence of God*, ed. D. Attwater, Paraclete Books, London, 1962, pp. 13, 16.

the liturgical books, together with Psalm and Scripture readings, intercession, and the like. A few may feel called to an almost exclusive concentration upon the Jesus Prayer, but this does not happen with most Indeed, many prefer simply to employ the Prayer in the "free" manner without using it "formally" in their "set" time of prayer; and there is nothing disquieting or incorrect about this. The "free" use may certainly exist without the "formal."

In the "formal" usage, as in the "free," there are no rigid rules, but variety and flexibility. No particular posture is essential. In Orthodox practice the Prayer is most usually recited when seated, but it may also be said standing or kneeling – and even, in cases of bodily weakness and physical exhaustion, when lying down. It is normally recited in more or less complete darkness or with the eyes closed, not with open eyes before an icon illuminated by candles or a votive lamp. *Starets* Silouan of Mount Athos (1866-1938), when saying the Prayer, used to stow his clock away in a cupboard so as not to hear it ticking, and then pull his thick woolen monastic cap over his eyes and ears.[15]

Darkness, however, can have a soporific effect! If we become drowsy as we sit or kneel reciting the Prayer, then we should stand up for a time, make the Sign of the Cross at the end of each Prayer, and then bend from the waist in a deep bow, touching the ground with the fingers of the right hand. We may even make a prostration each time, touching the ground with our forehead. When reciting the Prayer seated, we should ensure that the chair is not too restful or luxurious; preferably it should have no arms. In Orthodox monasteries a low stool is commonly used, without a back. The Prayer may also be recited standing with arms outstretched in the form of a cross.

---

[15] Archimandrite Sofrony, *The Undistorted Image: Staretz Silouan*, London, 1958, pp. 40–41.

A prayer-rope or rosary (*komvoschoinion*, *tchotki*), normally with a hundred knots, is often employed in conjunction with the Prayer, not primarily in order to count the number of times it is repeated, but rather as an aid to concentration and the establishment of a regular rhythm. It is a widespread fact of experience that, if we make some use of our hands as we pray, this will help to still our body and to gather us together into the act of prayer. But quantitative measurement, whether with a prayer-rope or in other ways, is on the whole not encouraged. It is true that, in the early part of *The Way of a Pilgrim*, great emphasis is laid by the *starets* on the precise number of times that the Prayer is to be said daily: 3,000 times, increasing to 6,000, and then to 12,000. The Pilgrim is commanded to say an exact number, neither more nor less. Such attention to quantity is altogether unusual. Possibly the point here is not the sheer quantity but the inner attitude of the Pilgrim: the *starets* wishes to test his obedience and readiness to fulfil an appointed task without deviation. More typical, however, is the advice of Bishop Theophane: "no not trouble about the number of times you say the Prayer. Let this be your sole concern, that it should spring up in your heart with quickening power like a fountain of living water. Expel entirely from your mind all thoughts of quantity."[16]

The Prayer is sometimes recited in groups, but more commonly alone; the words may be said aloud or silently. In Orthodox usage, when recited aloud it is spoken rather than chanted. There should be nothing forced or labored in the recitation. The words should not be formed with excessive emphasis or inner violence, but the Prayer should be allowed to establish its own rhythm and accentuation, so that in time it comes to "sing" within us by virtue of its

---

[16] Quoted in E. Behr–Sigel, "La Prière à Jésus ou le mystère de la spiritualité monastique orthodoxe," *Dieu Vivant* 8, 1947, p.81.

intrinsic melody. *Starets* Parfenii of Kiev likened the flowing movement of the Prayer to a gently murmuring stream.[17]

From all this it can be seen that the Invocation of the Name is a prayer for all seasons. It can be used by everyone, in every place and at every time. It is suitable for the "beginner" as well as the more experienced; it can be offered in company with others or alone; it is equally appropriate in the desert or the city, in surroundings of recollected tranquillity or in the midst of the utmost noise and agitation. It is never out of place.

Completeness

Theologically, as the Russian Pilgrim rightly claims, the Jesus Prayer "holds in itself the whole gospel truth"; it is a "summary of the Gospels."[18] In one brief sentence it embodies the two chief mysteries of the Christian faith, the Incarnation and the Trinity. It speaks, first, of the two natures of Christ the God-man (*Theanthropos*): of his humanity, for he is invoked by the human name, "Jesus," which his Mother Mary gave to him after his birth in Bethlehem; of his eternal Godhead, for he is also styled "Lord" and "Son of God." In the second place, the Prayer speaks by implication, although not explicitly, of the three Persons of the Trinity. While addressed to the second Person, Jesus, it points also to the Father, for Jesus is called "Son of God"; and the Holy Spirit is equally present in the Prayer, for "no one can say "Lord Jesus," except in the Holy Spirit" (I Cor 12:3). So the Jesus Prayer is both Christocentric and Trinitarian.

Devotionally, it is no less comprehensive. It embraces the two chief "moments" of Christian worship: the "moment" of adoration, of looking up to God's glory and reaching out to

---

[17] *The Art of Prayer*, p.110.
[18] *The Way of a Pilgrim*, trans. R. M. French, London, 1954, p.29.

145

him in love; and the "moment" of penitence, the sense of unworthiness and sin. There is a circular movement within the Prayer, a sequence of ascent and return. In the first half of the Prayer we rise up to God: "Lord Jesus Christ, Son of God . . ."; and then in the second half we return to ourselves in compunction: ". . . on me a sinner." "Those who have tasted the gift of the Spirit," it is stated in the Macarian Homilies, "are conscious of two things at the same time: on the one hand, of joy and consolation; on the other, of trembling and fear and mourning."[19] Such is the inner dialectic of the Jesus Prayer.

These two "moments" – the vision of divine glory and the consciousness of human sin – are united and reconciled in a third "moment" as we pronounce the word "mercy." "Mercy" denotes the bridging of the gulf between God's righteousness and the fallen creation. He who says to God "Have mercy," laments his own helplessness but voices at the same time a cry of hope. He speaks not only of sin but of its overcoming. He affirms that God in his glory accepts us though we are sinners, asking us in return to accept the fact that we are accepted. So the Jesus Prayer contains not only a call to repentance but an assurance of forgiveness and restoration. The heart of the Prayer – the actual name "Jesus" – bears precisely the sense of salvation: "Thou shalt call his name Jesus, for he shall save his people from their sins" (Mt 1 :21). While there is sorrow for sin in the Jesus Prayer, it is not a hopeless but a "joy-creating sorrow" in the phrase of St John Climacus († c. 649).

Such are among the riches, both theological and devotional, present in the Jesus Prayer; present, moreover, not merely in the abstract but in a vivifying and dynamic form. The special value of the Jesus Prayer lies in the fact that it makes these truths come alive, so that they are

---

[19] H. Berthold, *Makarios/Symeon, Reden und Briefe, Logos* B33, 2, 1: vol. ii, Berlin, 1973, p. 29.

apprehended not just externally and theoretically but with all the fullness of our being. To understand why the Jesus Prayer possesses such efficacy, we must turn to two further aspects: the power of the Name and the discipline of repetition.

The Power of the Name

"The Name of the Son of God is great and boundless, and up holds the entire universe." So it is affirmed in *The Shepherd of Hermas*,[20] nor shall we appreciate the role of the Jesus Prayer in Orthodox spirituality unless we feel some sense of the power and virtue of the divine Name. If the Jesus Prayer is more creative than other invocations, this is because it contains the Name of God.

In the Old Testament,[21] as in other ancient cultures, there is a close connection between someone's soul and his name. His personality, with its peculiarities and its energy, is in some sense present in his name. To know a person's name is to gain an insight into his nature, and thereby to acquire a relationship with him – even, perhaps, a certain control over him. That is why the mysterious messenger who wrestles with Jacob at the ford Jabbok refuses to disclose his name (Gen 32:29). The same attitude is reflected in the reply of the angel to Manoah, "Why askest thou thus after my name, seeing it is secret?" (Judg 13:18). A change of name indicates a decisive change in a person's life, as when Abram becomes Abraham (Gen 17:5), or Jacob becomes Israel (Gen 32:28). In the same way, Saul after his conversion becomes Paul (Acts 13:9); and a monk at his profession is given a new name, usually not of his own choosing, to indicate the radical renewal which he undergoes.

---

[20] *Similitudes*, ix, 14.
[21] See J. Pedersen, *Israel*, vol. i, London/Copenhagen, 1926, pp. 245–59; but compare J. Barr, "The Symbolism of Names in the Old Testament," *Bulletin of the John Rylands Library* 52, 1, 1969, pp. 11–29.

In the Hebrew tradition, to do a thing *in the name* of another, or to *invoke* and *call upon his name*, are acts of weight and potency. To invoke a person's name is to make that person effectively present. "One makes a name alive by mentioning it. The name immediately calls forth the soul it designates; therefore there is such deep significance in the very mention of a name."[22]

Everything that is true of human names is true to an incomparably higher degree of the divine Name. The power and glory of God are present and active in his Name. The Name of God is *numen praesens*, God with us, *Emmanuel*. Attentively and deliberately to invoke God's Name is to place oneself in his presence, to open oneself to his energy, to offer oneself as an instrument and a living sacrifice in his hands. So keen was the sense of the majesty of the divine Name in later Judaism that the *tetragrammaton* was not pronounced aloud in the worship of the synagogue: the Name of the Most High was considered too devastating to be spoken.[23]

This Hebraic understanding of the Name passes from the Old Testament into the New. Devils are cast out and men are healed through the Name of Jesus, for the Name is power. Once this potency of the Name is properly appreciated, many familiar passages acquire a fuller meaning and force: the clause in the Lord's Prayer, "Hallowed be thy Name"; Christ's promise at the Last Supper "Whatever you shall ask the Father in my Name, he will give it you" (John 16:23); his final command to the apostles: "Go therefore, and teach all nations, baptizing them in the Name of the Father, and of the Son, and of the Holy Spirit" (Mt 28:19); St Peter's proclamation that there is salvation only in "the Name of Jesus Christ of Nazareth" (Acts 4:10-12); the words of St Paul, "At the

---

[22] Pedersen, op. cit., p. 256.

[23] For the veneration of the Name among medieval Jewish Kabbalists, see Gershom G. Scholem, *Major Trends in Jewish Mysticism*, 3rd ed., London, 1955, pp. 132–3; and compare the treatment of this theme in the remarkable novel of Charles Williams, *All Hallows' Eve*, London, 1945.

Name of Jesus every knee should bow" (Phil 2:10); the new and secret name written on the white stone which is given to us in the Age to Come (Rev 2:17).

It is this biblical reverence for the Name that forms the basis and foundation of the Jesus Prayer. God's Name is intimately linked with his Person, and so the Invocation of the divine Name possesses a sacramental character, serving as an efficacious sign of his invisible presence and action. For the believing Christian today, as in apostolic times, the Name of Jesus is power. In the words of the two Elders of Gaza, St Barsanuphius and St John (sixth century), "The remembrance of the Name of God utterly destroys all that is evil."[24] "Flog your enemies with the Name of Jesus," urges St John Climacus, "for there is no weapon more powerful in heaven or on earth. . . . Let the remembrance of Jesus be united to your every breath, and then you will know the value of stillness."[25]

The Name is power, but a purely mechanical repetition will by itself achieve nothing. The Jesus Prayer is not a magic talisman. As in all sacramental operations, the human person is required to co-operate with God through active faith and ascetic effort. We are called to invoke the Name with recollection and inward vigilance, confining our minds within the words of the Prayer, conscious who it is that we are addressing and that responds to us in our heart. Such strenuous prayer is never easy in the initial stages, and is rightly described by the Fathers as a hidden martyrdom. St Gregory of Sinai speaks repeatedly of the "constraint and labor" undertaken by those who follow the Way of the Name; a "continual effort" is needed; they will be tempted to give up "because of the insistent pain that comes from the inward invocation of the intellect." "Your

---

[24] *Questions and Answers*, ed. Sotirios Schoinas, Volos, 1960, para. 693; trans. L. Regnault and P. Lemaire, Solesmes, 1972, para. 692.
[25] *Ladder*, 21 and 27, PG 88, 945C and 1112C.

shoulders will ache and you will often feel pain in your head," he warns, "but persevere persistently and with ardent longing, seeking the Lord in your heart."[26] Only through such patient faithfulness shall we discover the true power of the Name.

This faithful perseverance takes the form, above all, of attentive and frequent repetition. Christ told his disciples not to use "vain repetitions" (Mt 6:7); but the repetition of the Jesus Prayer, when performed with inward sincerity and concentration, is most emphatically not "vain." The act of repeatedly invoking the Name has a double effect: it makes our prayer more unified and at the same time more inward.

Unification

As soon as we make a serious attempt to pray in spirit and in truth, at once we become acutely conscious of our interior disintegration, of our lack of unity and wholeness. In spite of all our efforts to stand before God, thoughts continue to move restlessly and aimlessly through our head, like the buzzing of flies (Bishop Theophane) or the capricious leaping of monkeys from branch to branch (Ramakrishna). To contemplate means, first of all, to be present where one is – to be *here* and *now*. But usually we find ourselves unable to restrain our mind from wandering at random over time and space. We recall the past, we anticipate the future, we plan what to do next; people and places come before us in unending succession. We lack the power to gather ourselves into the one place where we should be – *here*, in the presence of God; we are unable to live fully in the only moment of time that truly exists – *now*, the immediate present. This interior disintegration is one of the tragic consequences of the Fall. The people who get

---

[26] See Kallistos Ware, "The Jesus Prayer in St Gregory of Sinai" (article cited in note 189 above), pp. 14–15.

things done, it has been justly observed, are the people who do one thing at a time. But to do one thing at a time is no mean achievement. While difficult enough in external work, it is harder still in the work of inner prayer.

What is to be done? How shall we learn to live in the present, in the eternal Now? How can we seize the *kairos*, the decisive moment" the moment of opportunity? It is precisely at this point that the Jesus Prayer can help. The repeated Invocation of the Name can bring us, by God's grace, from dividedness to unity, from dispersion and multiplicity to singleness. "To stop the continual jostling of your thoughts," says Bishop Theophane, "you must bind the mind with one thought, or the thought of One only."[27]

The ascetic Fathers, in particular Barsanuphius and John, distinguish two ways of combatting thoughts. The first method is for the "strong" or the "perfect." These can "contradict" their thoughts, that is, confront them face to face and repel them in direct battle. But for most of us such a method is too difficult and may, indeed, lead to actual harm. Direct confrontation, the attempt to uproot and expel thoughts by an effort of will, often serves merely to give greater strength to our imagination. Violently suppressed, our fantasies tend to return with increased force. Instead of fighting our thoughts directly and trying to eliminate them by an effort of will, it is wiser to turn aside and fix our attention elsewhere. Rather than gazing downwards into our turbulent imagination and concentrating on how to oppose our thoughts, we should look upwards to the Lord Jesus and entrust ourselves into his hands by invoking his Name; and the grace that acts through his Name will overcome the thoughts which we cannot obliterate by our own strength. Our spiritual strategy should be positive and not negative: instead of trying to empty our mind of what is evil, we should fill it with the thought of what is good. "Do not contradict the thoughts

---

[27] *The Art of Prayer*, p. 97.

151

suggested by your enemies," advise Barsanuphius and John, "for that is exactly what they want and they will not cease from troubling you. But turn to the Lord for help against them, laying before him your own powerlessness; for he is able to expel them and to reduce them to nothing."[28]

The Jesus Prayer, then, is a way of turning aside and looking elsewhere. Thoughts and images inevitably occur to us during prayer. We cannot stop them by a mere exertion of our will. We cannot simply turn off the internal television set. It is of little or no value to say to ourselves "Stop thinking"; we might as well say "Stop breathing'. "The rational mind cannot rest idle," says St Mark the Monk,[29] for thoughts keep filling it with ceaseless chatter. But while it lies beyond our power to make this chatter suddenly disappear, what we can do is to detach ourselves from it by "binding" our ever-active mind "with one thought, or the thought of One only" – the Name of Jesus. We cannot altogether halt the flow of thoughts, but through the Jesus Prayer we can disengage ourselves progressively from it, allowing it to recede into the background so that we become less and less aware of it.

According to Evagrius of Pontus (†399), "Prayer is a laying aside of thoughts."[30] *A laying aside:* not a savage conflict, not a furious repression, but a gentle yet persistent act of detachment. Through the repetition of the Name" we are helped to "lay aside," to "let go," our trivial or pernicious imaginings, and to replace them with the thought of Jesus. But, although the imagination and the discursive reasoning are not to be violently suppressed when saying the Jesus Prayer, they are certainly not to be actively encouraged. The Jesus Prayer is not a form of

---

[28] *Questions and Answers*, ed. Schoinas, para. 91; trans. Regnault and Lemaire, para. 166.
[29] *On Penitence*, 11, PG 65, 981B. The Greek text in Migne requires emendation here.
[30] *On Prayer*, 70, PG 79, 1181C.

meditation upon specific incidents in the life of Christ, or upon some saying or parable in the Gospels; still less is it a way of reasoning and inwardly debating about some theological truth such as the meaning of *homoousios* or the Chalcedonian Definition. In this regard, the Jesus Prayer is to be distinguished from the methods of discursive meditation popular in the West since the Counter Reformation (commended by Ignatius Loyola, François de Sales, Alphonsus Ligouri, and others).

As we invoke the Name, we should not deliberately shape in our minds any visual image of the Saviour. This is one of the reasons why we usually say the Prayer in darkness, rather than with our eyes open in front of an icon. "Keep your intellect free from colors, images and forms," urges St Gregory of Sinai; beware of the imagination (*phantasia*) in prayer otherwise you may find that you have become a *phantastes* instead of a *hesychastes*![31] "So as not to fall into illusion (*prelest*) while practising inner prayer," states St Nil Sorskii (†1508), "do not permit yourself any concepts, images or visions,"[32] "Hold no intermediate image between the intellect and the Lord when practising the Jesus prayer," Bishop Theophane writes. ". . . The essential part is to dwell in God" and this walking before God means that you live with the conviction ever before your consciousness that God is in you, as he is in everything: you live in the firm assurance that he sees all that is within you, knowing you better than you know yourself. This awareness of the eye of God looking at your inner being *must not he accompanied by any visual concept, but must he confined to a simple conviction or feeling.*"[33] Only when we invoke the Name in this way – not forming pictures of the Saviour but simply *feeling* his

---

[31] *How the hesychast should persevere in prayer,* 7, PG 150, 1340D.
[32] *The Art of Prayer,* p. 101.
[33] *The Art of Prayer,* p. 100.

presence – shall we experience the full power of the Jesus Prayer to integrate and unify.

The Jesus Prayer is thus a prayer in words, but because the words are so simple, so few and unvarying, the Prayer reaches out beyond words into the living silence of the Eternal. It is a way of achieving, with God's assistance, the kind of non-discursive, non-iconic prayer in which we do not simply make statements to or about God, in which we do not just form pictures of Christ in our imagination, but are "oned" with him in an all-embracing, unmediated encounter. Through the Invocation of the Name we feel his nearness with our spiritual senses, much as we feel the warmth with our bodily senses on entering a heated room. We know him, not through a series of successive images and concepts, but with the unified sensibility of the heart. So the Jesus Prayer concentrates us into the *here* and *now*, making us single-centered, one-pointed, drawing us from a multiplicity of thoughts to union with the one Christ "Through the remembrance of Jesus Christ," says St Philotheus of Sinai (?ninth–tenth century), "gather together your scattered intellect"[34] gather it together from the plurality of discursive thinking into the simplicity of love.

Many, on hearing that the Invocation of the Name is to be non-discursive and non-iconic, a means of transcending images and thoughts, may be tempted to conclude that any such manner of praying lies altogether beyond their capacities. To such it should be said: the Way of the Name is *not* reserved for a select few. It is within the reach of all. When you first embark on the Jesus Prayer, do not worry too much about expelling thoughts and mental pictures. As we have said already, let your strategy be positive, not negative. Call to mind, not what is to be excluded, but what is to be included. Do not think about your thoughts and how

---

[34] *Texts on Watchfulness*, 27: cf. G. E. H. Palmer, Philip Sherrard and Kallistos Ware, (trans.), *The Philokalia*, vol. iii, London, 1984, p. 27.

to shed them; think about Jesus. Concentrate your whole self, all your ardor and devotion, upon the person of the Saviour. Feel his presence. Speak to him with love. If your attention wanders, as undoubtedly it will, do not be discouraged; gently, without exasperation or inner anger, bring it back. If it wanders again and again, then again and yet again bring it back. Return to the center – to the living and personal center, Jesus Christ

Look on the Invocation, not so much as prayer emptied of thoughts, but as prayer filled with the Beloved. Let it be, in the richest sense of the word, a prayer of *affection* – although not of self-induced emotional excitement. For while the Jesus Prayer is certainly far more than "affective" prayer in the technical Western sense, it is with our loving affection that we do right to begin. Our inner attitude, as we commence the Invocation, is that of St Richard of Chichester:

> *O my merciful Redeemer, Friend and Brother,*
> *May I see thee more clearly,*
> *love thee more dearly,*
> *and follow thee more nearly.*

Without denying or diminishing the classic teaching of the Hesychast masters on the Jesus Prayer as a "shedding of thoughts," it has to be acknowledged that over the centuries most Eastern Christians have used the Prayer simply as an expression of their tender, loving trust in Jesus the Divine Companion. And there is surely no harm in that.

Inwardness

The repeated Invocation of the Name, by making our prayer more unified, makes it at the same time more inward, more a part of ourselves not something that we *do* at particular moments, but something that we *are* all the time; not an occasional act but a continuing state. Such praying becomes truly prayer of the *whole person*, in which the words and meaning of the prayer are fully identified with the one who prays. All this is well expressed by Paul Evdokimov (1901-1970): "In the catacombs the image that recurs most frequently is the figure of a woman in prayer, the *Orans*. It represents the only true attitude of the human soul. It is not enough to *possess* prayer: we must *become* prayer – prayer incarnate. It is not enough to have moments of praise; our whole life, every act and every gesture, even a smile, must become a hymn of adoration, an offering, a prayer. We must offer not what we *have* but what we *are*."[35] That is what the world needs above all else: not people who *say* prayers with greater or less regularity, but people who *are* prayers.

The kind of prayer that Evdokimov is here describing may be defined more exactly as "prayer of the heart." In Orthodoxy, as in other traditions, prayer is commonly distinguished under three headings, which are to be regarded as interpenetrating levels rather than successive stages: prayer of the lips (oral prayer); prayer of the *nous*, the mind or intellect (mental prayer); prayer of the heart (or of the intellect in the heart). The Invocation of the Name begins, like any other prayer, as an oral prayer, in which words are spoken by the tongue through a deliberate effort of will. At the same time, once more by a deliberate effort, we concentrate our mind upon the meaning of what the tongue says. In course of time and with the help of God our prayer grows more inward. The participation of the mind becomes more intense and spontaneous, while the sounds uttered by the tongue become less important; perhaps for a time they cease altogether and the Name is invoked silently, without any movement of the lips, by the mind alone. When this occurs, we have passed by God's grace from the first level to the second. Not that vocal invocation ceases altogether,

---

[35] *Sacrement de l'amour. Le mystère conjugal à la lumière de la tradition orthodoxe*, Paris, 1962, p. 83.

for there will be times when even the most "advanced" in inner prayer will wish to call upon the Lord Jesus aloud. (And who, indeed, can claim to be "advanced"? We are all of us "beginners" in the things of the Spirit.)

But the journey inwards is not yet complete. A person is far more than the conscious mind; besides the brain and reasoning faculties there are the emotions and affections, the aesthetic sensitivity, together with the deep instinctive layers of the personality. All these have a function to perform in prayer, for the whole person is called to share in the total act of worship. Like a drop of ink that falls on blotting paper, the act of prayer should spread steadily outwards from the conscious and reasoning center of the brain, until it embraces every part of ourselves.

In more technical terms, this means that we are called to advance from the second level to the third: from "prayer of the intellect" to "prayer of the intellect in the heart." "Heart" in this context is to be understood in the Semitic and biblical rather than the modern Western sense, as signifying not just the emotions and affections but the totality of the human person. The heart is the primary organ of our identity, it is our inner-most being, "the very deepest and truest self, not attained except through sacrifice, through death."[36] According to Boris Vysheslavtsev, it is "the center not only of consciousness but of the unconscious, not only of the soul but of the spirit, not only of the spirit but of the body, not only of the comprehensible but of the incomprehensible; in one word, it is the absolute center."[37] Interpreted in this way, the heart is far more than a material organ in the body; the physical heart is an outward symbol of the boundless

---

[36] Richard Kehoe OP, "The Scriptures as Word of God," *The Eastern Churches Quarterly* viii, 1947, supplementary issue on "Tradition and Scripture," p. 78.

[37] Quoted in John B. Dunlop, *Staretz Amvrosy: Model for Dostoevsky's Staretz Zossima*, Belmont, Mass., 1972, p. 22.

spiritual potentialities of the human creature, made in the image of God, called to attain his likeness.

To accomplish the journey inwards and to attain true prayer, it is required of us to enter into this "absolute center," that is, to descend from the intellect into the heart. More exactly, we are called to descend not from but *with* the intellect. The aim is not just "prayer of the heart" but "prayer of the intellect in the heart," for our varied forms of understanding, including our reason, are a gift from God and are to be used in his service, not rejected. This "union of the intellect with the heart" signifies the reintegration of our fallen and fragmented nature, our restoration to original wholeness. Prayer of the heart is a return to Paradise, a reversal of the Fall, a recovery of the *status ante peccatum*. This means that it is an eschatological reality, a pledge and anticipation of the Age to Come – something which, in this present age, is never fully and entirely realized.

Those who, however imperfectly, have achieved some measure of "prayer of the heart," have begun to make the transition about which we spoke earlier – the transition from "strenuous" to "self-acting" prayer, from the prayer which I say to the prayer which "says itself" or, rather, which Christ says in me. For the heart has a double significance in the spiritual life: it is both the center of the human being and the point of meeting between the human being and God. It is both the place of self-knowledge, where we see ourselves as we truly are, and the place of self-transcendence, where we understand our nature as a temple of the Holy Trinity, where the image comes face to face with the Archetype. In the "inner sanctuary" of our own heart we find the ground of our being and so cross the mysterious frontier between the created and the Uncreated. "There are unfathomable depths within the heart," state the Macarian Homilies. ". . . God is there with the angels, light and life are there, the kingdom and the apostles, the heavenly cities and the treasures of grace: all things are there."[38]

Prayer of the heart, then, designates the point where "my" action, "my" prayer, becomes explicitly identified with the continuous action of Another in me. It is no longer prayer to Jesus but the prayer of Jesus himself. This transition from "strenuous" to "self-acting" prayer is strikingly indicated in *The Way of a Pilgrim*: "Early one morning the Prayer woke me up as it were."[39] Hitherto the Pilgrim has been "saying the Prayer"; now he finds that the Prayer "says itself," even when he is asleep, for it has become united to the prayer of God within him. Yet even so he does not consider that he has as yet attained prayer of the heart in its fullness.

Readers of *The Way of a Pilgrim* may gain the impression that this passage from oral prayer to prayer of the heart is easily achieved, almost in a mechanical and automatic fashion. The Pilgrim, so it seems, attains self-acting prayer in a matter of a few weeks. It needs to be emphasized that his experience, while not unique,[40] is altogether exceptional. More usually prayer of the heart comes, if at all, only after a lifetime of ascetic striving. There is a real danger that, in the early stages of the Jesus Prayer, we may too readily assume that we are passing from oral prayer to prayer of the heart. We may perhaps be tempted to imagine that we have already attained wordless prayer of silence, when in fact we are not really praying at all but have merely lapsed into vacant drowsiness or waking sleep. To

---

[38] *Hom.* xv. 32 and xliii. 7, ed. Dörries/Klostermann/Kroeger, Berlin 1964, pp. 146, 289.

[39] *The Way of a Pilgrim*, p. 14.

[40] *Starets* Silouan of Mount Athos had only been practising the Jesus Prayer for three weeks before it descended into his heart and became unceasing. His biographer, Archimandrite Sofrony, rightly points out that this was a "sublime and rare gift"; not until later did Father Silouan come to appreciate how unusual it was, *The Undistorted Image*, p. 24. For further discussion of this question, see Kallistos Ware, "'Pray without Ceasing': The Ideal of Continual Prayer in Eastern Monasticism," *Eastern Churches Review* ii, 1969, pp. 259–61.

guard against this, our teachers in the Hesychast tradition insist upon the need for strenuous effort when first embarking on the Jesus Prayer. They emphasize how important it is to concentrate full attention upon the recitation of the actual words, rather than to form high ambitions about prayer of the heart. Here, for example, is the advice given by a noted spiritual father of Mount Athos, *Geron* Joseph of New Skete (died 1959):

> The work of inner prayer consists in forcing yourself to say the prayer with your mouth continually, without ceasing . . . Attend only to the words "Lord Jesus Christ, have mercy on me.". . . . Just say the Prayer aloud, without interruption. . . . All your effort must be centered on the tongue, until you start to grow accustomed to the Prayer.[41]

The significance attached here to the power of the spoken word is indeed striking. As St John Climacus tells us, "Struggle to lift up, or rather, to enclose your thought within the *words* of your prayer."[42] But of course we never think exclusively about the words on their own; always we are conscious also of the person of Jesus whom our words invoke.

Prayer of the heart, when and if it is granted, comes as the free gift of God, which he bestows as he wills. It is not the inevitable effect of some technique. St Isaac the Syrian (seventh century) underlines the extreme rarity of the gift when he says that "scarcely one in ten thousand" is counted worthy of the gift of pure prayer, and he adds: "As for the mystery that lies beyond pure prayer, there is scarcely to be found a single person in each generation who has drawn near to this knowledge of God's grace."[43] One in ten thousand, one in a generation: while sobered by this warning, we should not be unduly discouraged. The path

---

[41] *Ekphrasis monastikis empeirias*, Monastery of Philotheou, Holy Mountain, 1979, pp. 25 28.
[42] *Ladder*, 28, PG 88, 1132C.
[43] *Mystic Treatises by Isaac of Nineveh*, translated by A. J. Wensinck, Amsterdam 1923, p. 113.

to the inner kingdom lies open before all, and all alike may travel some way along it. In the present age, few experience with any fullness the deeper mysteries of the heart, but very many receive in a more humble and intermittent way true glimpses of what is signified by spiritual prayer.

Breathing exercises

It is time to consider a controversial topic, where the teaching of the Byzantine Hesychasts is often misinterpreted – the role of the body in prayer.

The heart, it has been said, is the primary organ of our being, the point of convergence between mind and matter, the center alike of our physical constitution and our psychic and spiritual structure. Since the heart has this twofold aspect, at once visible and invisible, prayer of the heart is prayer of body as well as soul: only if it includes the body can it be truly prayer of the whole person. A human being, in the biblical view, is a psychosomatic totality – not a soul imprisoned in a body and seeking to escape, but an integral unity of the two. The body is not just an obstacle to be overcome, a lump of matter to be ignored, but it has a positive part to play in the spiritual life and it is endowed with energies that can be harnessed for the work of prayer. If this is true of prayer in general, it is true in a more specific way of the Jesus Prayer, since this is an invocation addressed precisely to God Incarnate, to the Word made flesh. Christ at his Incarnation took not only a human mind and will but a human body, and so he has made the *flesh* into an inexhaustible source of sanctification. How can this flesh, which the God-man has made Spirit-bearing, participate in the Invocation of the Name and in the prayer of the intellect in the heart?

To assist such participation, and as an aid to concentration, the Hesychasts evolved a "physical technique." Every psychic activity, they realized, has repercussions on the physical and bodily level; depending on our inner state we grow hot or cold, we breathe faster or more slowly, the rhythm of our heart-beats quickens or decelerates, and so on. Conversely, each alteration in our physical condition reacts adversely or positively on our psychic activity. If, then, we can learn to control and regulate certain of our physical processes, this can be used to strengthen our inner concentration in prayer. Such is the basic principle underlying the Hesychast "method." In detail, the physical technique has three main aspects:

i) *External posture.* St Gregory of Sinai advises sitting on a low stool, about nine inches high; the head and shoulders should be bowed, and the eyes fixed on the place of the heart. He recognizes that this will prove exceedingly uncomfortable after a time. Some writers recommend a yet more exacting posture, with the head held between the knees, following the example of Elijah on Mount Carmel.[44]

ii) *Control of the breathing.* The breathing is to be made slower and at the same time coordinated with the rhythm of the Prayer. Often the first part, "Lord Jesus Christ, Son of God," is said while drawing in the breath, and the second part" "have mercy on me a sinner," while breathing out. Other methods are possible. The recitation of the Prayer may also be synchronized with the beating of the heart.

iii) *Inward exploration.* Just as the aspirant in Yoga is taught to concentrate his thought in specific parts of his body, so the Hesychast concentrates his thought in the cardiac center. While inhaling through his nose and propelling his breath down into his lungs, he makes his intellect "descend" with the breath and he "searches"

---

[44] "Elijah climbed to the crest of Carmel. There he crouched to the ground with his face between his knees," 1 Kings 18:42. For an illustration of a hesychast praying in this position, from a twelfth century MS of John Climacus, *The Ladder of Divine Ascent*, see *The Study of Spirituality*, ed. Cheslyn Jones, Geoffrey Wainwright and Edward Yarnold SJ, SPCK, London, 1986, plate 3, following p. 194.

inwardly for the place of the heart. Exact instructions concerning this exercise are not committed to writing for fear they should be misunderstood; the details of the process are so delicate that the personal guidance of an experienced master is *indispensable*. The beginner who, in the absence of such guidance, attempts to search for the cardiac center, is in danger of directing his thought unawares into the area which lies immediately below the heart – into the abdomen, that is, and the entrails. The effect on his prayer is disastrous, for this lower region is the source of the carnal thoughts and sensations which pollute the mind and the heart.[45]

For obvious reasons the utmost discretion is necessary when interfering with instinctive bodily activities such as the drawing of breath or the beating of the heart. Misuse of the physical technique can damage someone's health and disturb his mental equilibrium; hence the importance of a reliable master. If no such *starets* is available, it is best for the beginner to restrict himself simply to the actual recitation of the Jesus Prayer, without troubling at all about the rhythm of his breath or his heart-beats. More often than not he will find that, without any conscious effort on his part, the words of the Invocation adapt themselves spontaneously to the movement of his breathing. If this does not in fact happen, there is no cause for alarm; let him continue quietly with the work of mental invocation.

The physical techniques are in any case no more than an accessory, an aid which has proved helpful to some but which is in no sense obligatory upon all. The Jesus Prayer can be practised in its fullness without any physical

---

[45] For further bibliography on the control of the breathing, see Kallistos Ware, "The Jesus Prayer in St Gregory of Sinai" (cited above), p. 14, note 55. On the various physical centres and their spiritual implications, see Father Anthony Bloom (now Metropolitan of Sourozh), *Asceticism (Somatopsychic Techniques)*, The Guild of Pastoral Psychology, Guild Lecture No. 95, London, 1957.

methods at all. St Gregory Palamas (1296-1359), while regarding the use of physical techniques as theologically defensible, treated such methods as something secondary and suited mainly for beginners.[46] For him, as for all the Hesychast masters, the essential thing is not the external control of the breathing but the inner and secret Invocation of the Lord Jesus.

Orthodox writers in the last 150 years have in general laid little emphasis upon the physical techniques. The counsel given by Bishop Ignatii Brianchaninov (1807-67) is typical:

> We advise our beloved brethren not to try to establish this technique within them, if it does not reveal itself of its own accord. Many, wishing to learn it by experience, have damaged their lungs and gained nothing. The essence of the matter consists in the union of the mind with the heart during prayer, and this is achieved by the grace of God in its own time, determined by God. The breathing technique is fully replaced by the unhurried enunciation of the Prayer, by a short rest or pause at the end, each time it is said, by gentle and unhurried breathing, and by the enclosure of the mind in the words of the Prayer. By means of these aids we can easily attain to a certain degree of attention.[47]

As regards the speed of recitation, Bishop Ignatii suggests:

> To say the Jesus Prayer a hundred time attentively and without haste, about half an hour is needed, but some ascetics require even longer. Do not say the prayers hurriedly, one immediately after another. Make a short pause after each prayer, and so help the mind to concentrate. Saying the Prayer without pauses distracts the mind. Breathe with care, gently and slowly.[48]

Beginners in the use of the Prayer will probably prefer a somewhat faster pace than is here proposed – perhaps twenty minutes for a hundred prayers. In the Greek

---

[46] *Triads in defence of the Holy Hesychasts*, I, ii, 7, ed. J. Meyendorff, Louvain 1959, vol. i, p. 97.

[47] *The Arena. An Offering to Contemporary Monasticism*, translated by Archimandrite Lazarus, Madras 1970, p. 84 (translation slightly altered).

[48] Op. cit., p. 81.

tradition there are teachers who recommend a far brisker rhythm; the very rapidity of the Invocation, so they maintain, helps to hold the mind attentive.

Striking parallels exist between the physical techniques recommended by the Byzantine Hesychasts and those employed in Hindu Yoga and in Sùfism.[49] How far are the similarities the result of mere coincidence, of an independent though analogous development in two separate traditions? If there is a direct relation between Hesychasm and Sùfism – and some of the parallels are so close that mere coincidence seems excluded – which side has been borrowing from the other? Here is a fascinating field for research, although the evidence is perhaps too fragmentary to permit any definite conclusion. One point, however, should not be forgotten. Besides similarities, there are also differences. All pictures have frames, and all picture-frames have certain features in common: yet the pictures within the frames may be utterly different. What matters is the picture, not the frame. In the case of the Jesus Prayer, the physical techniques are as it were the frame, while the mental invocation of Christ is the picture within the frame. The "frame" of the Jesus Prayer certainly resembles various non-Christian "frames," but this should not make us insensitive to the uniqueness of the picture within, to the distinctively Christian content of the Prayer. The essential point in the Jesus Prayer is not the act of repetition in itself, not how we sit or breathe, but *to whom* we speak; and in this instance the words are addressed unambiguously to the Incarnate Saviour Jesus Christ, Son of God and Son of Mary.

The existence of a physical technique in connection with the Jesus Prayer should not blind us as to the Prayer's true

---

[49] See Louis Gardet, "Un problème de mystique comparée: la mention du nom divin (dhikr) dans la mystique musulmane," *Revue Thomiste*, lii, 1952, pp. 642–79; liii, 1953, pp. 197–216; reprinted in G. C. Anawati and L. Gardet, *Mystique musulmane: aspects et tendances – expériences et techniques*, Paris, 1961, pp. 187–256.

character. The Jesus Prayer is not just a device to help us concentrate or relax. It is not simply a piece of "Christian Yoga," a type of "Transcendental Meditation," or a "Christian mantra," even though some have tried to interpret it in this way. It is, on the contrary, an invocation specifically *addressed to another person* – to God made man, Jesus Christ, our personal Saviour and Redeemer. The Jesus Prayer, therefore, is far more than an isolated method or technique. It exists within a certain context, and if divorced from that context it loses its proper meaning.

The context of the Jesus Prayer is first of all one of *faith*. The Invocation of the Name presupposes that the one who says the Prayer believes in Jesus Christ as Son of God and Saviour. Behind the repetition of a form of words there must exist a living faith in the Lord Jesus in who he is and in what he has done for me personally. Perhaps the faith in many of us is very uncertain and faltering; perhaps it coexists with doubt; perhaps we often find ourselves compelled to cry out in company with the father of the lunatic child, "Lord, I believe: help my unbelief" (Mk 9:24). But at least there should be some *desire* to believe; at least there should be, amidst all the uncertainty, a spark of love for the Jesus whom as yet we know so imperfectly.

Secondly, the context of the Jesus Prayer is one of *community*. We do not invoke the Name as separate individuals, relying solely upon our own inner resources, but as members of the community of the Church. Writers such as St Barsanuphius, St Gregory of Sinai or Bishop Theophane took it for granted that those to whom they commended the Jesus Prayer were baptized Christians, regularly participating in the Church's sacramental life through Confession and Holy Communion. Not for one moment did they envisage the Invocation of the Name as a substitute for the sacraments, but they assumed that anyone using it would be a practising and communicant member of the Church. Yet today, in this present epoch of restless curiosity and ecclesiastical disintegration, there are in fact many who use the Jesus Prayer without belonging to any Church, possibly without having a clear faith either in the Lord Jesus or in anything else. Are we to condemn them? Are we to forbid them the use of the Prayer? Surely not, so long as they are sincerely searching for the Fountain of Life. Jesus condemned no one except hypocrites. But, in all humility and acutely aware of our own faithlessness, we are bound to regard the situation of such people as anomalous, and to warn them of this fact.

The Journey's End

The aim of the Jesus Prayer, as of all Christian prayer, is that our praying should become increasingly identified with the prayer offered by Jesus the High Priest within us, that our life should become one with his life, our breathing with the Divine Breath that sustains the universe. The final objective may aptly be described by the Patristic term *theosis*, "deification" or "divinization." In the words of Archpriest Sergei Bulgakov, "The Name of Jesus, present in the human heart, confers upon it the power of deification."[50] "The Logos became man," says St Athanasius, "that we might become god."[51] He who is God by nature took our humanity, that we humans might share by grace in his divinity, becoming "partakers of the divine nature" (2 Pet 1:4). The Jesus Prayer, addressed to the Logos Incarnate, is a means of realizing within ourselves this mystery of *theosis*, whereby human persons attain the true likeness of God.

The Jesus Prayer, by uniting us to Christ, helps us to share in the mutual indwelling or *perichoresis* of the three Persons of the Holy Trinity. The more the Prayer becomes

---

[50] *The Orthodox Church*, London 1935, p. 170 (translation altered).
[51] *On the Incarnation*, 54.

a part of ourselves, the more we enter into the movement of love which passes unceasingly between Father, Son, and Holy Spirit. Of this love St Isaac the Syrian has written with great beauty:

> Love is the kingdom of which our Lord spoke symbolically when he promised his disciples that they would eat in his kingdom: "You shall eat and drink at the table of my kingdom." What should they eat, if not love? . . . When we have reached love, we have reached God and our way is ended: we have passed over to the island that lies beyond the world, where is the Father with the Son and the Holy Spirit: to whom be glory and dominion.[52]

In the Hesychast tradition, the mystery of *theosis* has most often taken the outward form of a vision of light. This light which the saints behold in prayer is neither a symbolical light of the intellect, nor yet a physical and created light of the senses. It is nothing less than the divine and uncreated Light of the Godhead, which shone from Christ at his Transfiguration on Mount Tabor and which will illumine the whole world at his second coming on the Last Day. Here is a characteristic passage on the Divine Light taken from St Gregory Palamas. He is describing the Apostle's vision when he was caught up into the third heaven (2 Cor 12:2-4):

> Paul saw a light without limits below or above or to the sides; he saw no limit whatever to the light that appeared to him and shone around him, but it was like a sun infinitely brighter and vaster than the universe; and in the midst of this sun he himself stood, having become nothing but eye.[53]

Such is the vision of glory to which we may approach through the Invocation of the Name.

The Jesus Prayer causes the brightness of the Transfiguration to penetrate into every corner of our life. Constant

---

[52] *Mystic Treatises*, trans. Wensinck, pp. 211–12.
[53] *Triads in defence of the Holy Hesychasts*, I, iii, 21, ed. Meyendorff, vol. i, p. 157.

repetition has two effects upon the anonymous author of *The Way of a Pilgrim*. First, it transforms his relationship with the material creation around him, making all things transparent, changing them into a sacrament of God's presence. He writes:

> When I prayed with my heart, everything around me seemed delightful and marvellous. The trees, the grass, the birds, the earth, the air, the light seemed to be telling me that they existed for man's sake, that they witnessed to the love of God for man, that everything proved the love of God for man, that all things prayed to God and sang his praise. Thus it was that I came to understand what *The Philokalia* calls "the knowledge of the speech of all creatures.". I felt a burning love for Jesus and for all God's creatures.[54]

In the words of Father Bulgakov, "Shining through the heart, the light of the Name of Jesus illuminates all the universe."[55]

In the second place, the Prayer transfigures the Pilgrim's relation not only with the material creation but with other humans:

> Again I started off on my wanderings. But now I did not walk along as before, filled with care. The Invocation of the Name of Jesus gladdened my way. Everybody was kind to me, it was as though everyone loved me. . . . If anyone harms me I have only to think, "How sweet is the Prayer of Jesus!" and the injury and the anger alike pass away and I forget it all.[56]

"Inasmuch as you have done it unto one of the least of these my brethren, you have done it unto me" (Matt. 25:40). The Jesus Prayer helps us to see Christ in each one, and each one in Christ

The Invocation of the Name is in this way joyful rather than penitential, world-affirming rather than world-denying.

---

[54] *The Way of a Pilgrim*, pp. 3 1–2, 41.
[55] *The Orthodox Church*, p. 171.
[56] *The Way of a Pilgrim*, pp. 17–18.

To some, hearing about the Jesus Prayer for the first time, it may appear that to sit alone in the darkness with eyes closed, constantly repeating ". . . have mercy on me," is a gloomy and despondent way of praying. And they may also be tempted to regard it as self-centered and escapist, introverted, an evasion of responsibility to the human community at large. But this would be a grave misunderstanding. For those who have actually made the Way of the Name their own, it turns out to be not sombre and oppressive but a source of liberation and healing. The warmth and joyfulness of the Jesus Prayer is particularly evident in the writings of St Hesychius of Sinai (?eighth–ninth century):

> Through persistence in the Jesus Prayer the intellect attains a state of sweetness and peace. . . .
>
> The more the rain falls on the earth, the softer it makes it; similarly, the more we call upon Christ's Holy Name, the greater the rejoicing and exultation it brings to the earth of our heart. . . .
>
> The sun rising over the earth creates the daylight; and the venerable and Holy Name of the Lord Jesus, shining continually in the mind, gives birth to countless thoughts radiant as the sun.[57]

Moreover, so far from turning our backs on others and repudiating God's creation when we say the Jesus Prayer, we are in fact affirming our commitment to our neighbor and our sense of the value of everyone and everything in God. "Acquire inner peace," said St Seraphim of Sarov (1759-1833), "and thousands around you will find their salvation." By standing in Christ's presence even for no more than a few moments of each day, invoking his Name, we deepen and transform all the remaining moments of the day, rendering ourselves available to others, effective and creative, in a way that we could not otherwise be. And if we also use the Prayer in a "free" manner throughout the day,

---

[57] *On Watchfulness and Holiness*, 7, 41, 196: cf. Palmer, Sherrard and Ware, *The Philokalia*, vol. i, London, 1979, pp. 163, 169, 197.

this enables us to "set the divine seal on the world," to adopt a phrase of Dr. Nadejda Gorodetzky (1901-85):

> We can apply this Name to people, books, flowers, to all things we meet, see or think. The Name of Jesus may become a mystical key to the world, an instrument of the hidden offering of everything and everyone, setting the divine seal on the world. One might perhaps speak here of the priesthood of all believers. In union with our High Priest, we implore the Spirit: Make my prayer into a sacrament.[58]

"We can apply this Name to people. . . ." Here Dr. Gorodetzky suggests a possible answer to a question that is often raised: Can the Jesus Prayer be used as a form of intercession? The reply must be that, in the strict sense, it is distinct from intercessory prayer. As an expression of non-discursive, non-iconic "waiting upon God," it does not involve the explicit recalling and mention of particular names. We simply turn to Jesus. It is true, of course, that in turning to Jesus we do not thereby turn away from our fellow humans. All those whom we love are already embraced in his heart, loved by him infinitely more than by us, and so in the end through the Jesus Prayer we find them all again in him; invoking the Name, we enter more and more fully into Christ's overflowing love for the entire world. But if we are following the traditional Hesychast pattern of the Jesus Prayer, we do not bring others before him specifically by name, or hold them deliberately in our mind, as we recite the Invocation.

All this, however, does not exclude the possibility of also giving to the Jesus Prayer an intercessory dimension. On occasion, alike in the "free" and the "formal" use, we may feel moved to "apply" the Name to one or more particular persons, invoking Jesus upon them as we say ". . . have mercy on us," or even including the actual name or names, ". . . have mercy on John." Even if this is not exactly what

---

[58] "The Prayer of Jesus," *Blackfriars* xxiii, 1942, p. 76.

the Hesychast texts envisage, it is surely a legitimate and helpful extension to the practice of the Jesus Prayer. The Way of the Name has a wideness, a generosity, not to be confined within rigid and unvarying rules.

"Prayer is action; to pray is to be highly effective."[59] Of no prayer is this more true than of the Jesus Prayer. While it is singled out for particular mention in the office of monastic profession as a prayer for monks and nuns,[60] it is equally a prayer for laymen, for married couples, for doctors and psychiatrists, for social workers and bus conductors. The Invocation of the Name, practised aright, involves each one more deeply in his or her appointed task, making each more efficient in his actions, not cutting him off from others but linking him to them, rendering him sensitive to their fears and anxieties in a way that he never was before. The Jesus Prayer makes each into a "man for others," a living instrument of God's peace, a dynamic center of reconciliation.

---

[59] Tito Colliander, *The Way of the Ascetics*, p. 71.

[60] At the clothing of a monk, in both the Greek and the Russian practice, it is the custom to give him a prayer-rope (*komvoschoinion*). In the Russian use the abbot says the following as it is handed over: "Take, brother, the sword of the Spirit, which is the Word of God, for continual prayer to Jesus; for you must always have the Name of the Lord Jesus in mind, in heart and on your lips, ever saying: Lord Jesus Christ, Son of God, have mercy on me a sinner." See N. F. Robinson SSJE, *Monasticism in the Orthodox Churches*, London/Milwaukee, 1916, pp. 159–60. Note the usual distinction between three levels of prayer: lips, mind, heart.

Further Reading

"A Monk of the Eastern Church" [Archimandrite Lev Gillet], *The Jesus Prayer*. New edition, St. Vladimir's Seminary Press, New York, 1987. The best introduction to the history of the Prayer, with valuable suggestions on its practical use and detailed bibliography.

Irénée Hausherr sj, *The Name of Jesus*. Cistercian Studies Series 44: Kalamzoo, 1978. Historical; an authoritative scholarly treatment.

The Way of a Pilgrim, tr. R. M. French. London, 1954. A classic nineteenth-century Russian text.

Bishop Ignatii Brianchaninov, *On the Prayer of Jesus*, tr. Fr. Lazarus. London, 1952. Quotes many earlier authors.

Mother Maria, *The Jesus Prayer*. Library of Orthodox Thinking, Greek Orthodox Monastery of the Assumption, Normanby, 1972. Talks given by an Orthodox nun to an Anglican Benedictine Community.

Wendy Robinson, *Exploring Silence*. Fairacres Publication 36, Oxford, 1974. On prayer as listening.

Kallistos Ware, *The Orthodox Way*. Mowbrays, London and Oxford, 1979. A popular general account of the doctrine, worship and life of Orthodox Christians, which raises the basic issues of Christian theology and prayer.

Appendix

BIBLIOGRAPHY

I. Introduction to Orthodoxy and to Orthodox Spirituality

Bulgakov, Sergius, *The Orthodox Church*, Three Hierarchs Seminary Press, Maitland, Florida, 1935.

Bouyer, Louis, Histoire de la spiritualaité anglicane et orthodoxe, Aubier, Paris, 1965.

Clement, Olivier, *Sources*, Stock, Paris, 1982.

————, *L'Eglise orthodoxe*, Presses Universitaires de France, Paris, 1985.

Evdokimov, Paul, *L'Orthodoxie*, Delachaux et Niestlé, Neuchâtel, 1959.

Lossky, Vladimir, *The Mystical Theology of the Eastern Church*, St Vladimir's Seminary Press, New York, 1976.

A Monk of the Eastern Church, *Orthodox Spirituality*, St Vladimir's Seminary Press, New York, 1978.

Nellas, Panayiotis, *Le Vivant divinisé*, Cerf, Paris, 1989.

Ware, Kallistos, *The Orthodox Way*, St Vladimir's Seminary Press, New York, 1979.

Yannaras, Christos, *La foi vivante de l'Eglise*, Cerf, Paris, 1989.

II. The Church of the First Centuries

Bouyer, Louis, *Histoire de la spiritualité du Nouveau Testament et des Pères*, Aubier, Paris, 1960.

Cabasilas, Nicolas, *The Life in Christ*, St Vladimir's Seminary Press, New York, 1974.

Jaubert, Annie, Les Premiers Chrétiens, Seuil, Paris, 1967.

Early Christian Writings: The Apostolic Fathers, Penguin Books, New York, 1968.

Lot-Borodine, Myrrha, *La Déification de l'homme*, Cerf, Paris, 1970.

III. The Spirituality of Primitive Monasticism

The Wisdom of the Desert Fathers, Fairacres Publications 48, Oxford, 1975.

St Athanasius the Great, *The Life of Anthony*, Paulist Press, New York, 1980.

St John Climacus, *The Ladder of Divine Ascent*, Eastern Orthodox Books, Willits, California, 1959.

Deseille, Placide, *L'Evangile au désert: Origines et développement de la spiritualité monastique*, OEIL-YMCA Press, Paris, 1985.

L'Esprit du monachisme pachômien, Bellefontaine, 1979.

Guillaumont, Antoine, *Aux origines du monachisme chrétien*, Bellefontaine, 1979.

IV. Hesychasm and the Prayer of the Heart

Texts:

Hausherr, Irénée, *La Méthode d'oraison hésychaste*, Orientalia Christiana, Rome, 1927.

Palamas, Gregory, *Homélies*, OEIL-YMCA Press, Paris, 1987.

Petite Philocalie de la Prière du cœur, Seuil, collection "Livre de vie," Paris, 1968.

The Philokalia, vol I, Faber and Faber, London, 1979.

St Symeon the New Theologian, *Œuvres*, Sources Chrétiennes 51, 96, 104, 113, 156, 174, 179, 196.

Studies:

Behr-Sigel, Elisabeth, *Douloureuse joie*, Bellefontaine, 1974.

Hausherr, Irénée, *Solitude et Vie contemplative selon l'hésychasme*, Bellefontaine, 1981.

Lossky, Vladimir, *The Vision of God*, The Faith Press, London, 1963.

A Monk of the Eastern Church, *The Jesus Prayer*, New York, 1967.

V. The Christian Spirituality of Ancient Russia

Arseniev, Nicholas, *Russian Piety*, The Faith Press, London, 1964.

Behr-Sigel, Elisabeth, *Prière et Sainteté dans l'Eglise russe*, Bellefontaine, 1982.

——, "Monachisme russe" and "Nil Sorsky," *Dictionnaire de spiritualité*, Beauchesne, Paris.

Gorainoff, Irina, *Séraphin de Sarov*, Desclée de Brouwer, Paris, 1980.

————, *Les Fols en Christ*, Desclée de Brouwer, Paris, 1983.

Maloney, George, *Russian Hesychasm: The Spirituality of Nil Sorsky*, Mouton, The Hague, 1973.

Saint Nil Sorsky, French texts, Bellefontaine, 1986.

Smolitsch, Igor, *Moines de la Sainte Russie*, Mame, Paris, 1967.

Mille an de christianisme en Russie, texts of an international symposium, Œil-YMCA Press, Paris, 1989.

VI. Aspects of Orthodox Spirituality in the Eighteenth and Twentieth Centuries, in Russia and Elsewhere

Brianchaninov, Ignatius, *On the Prayer of Jesus*, John M. Watkins, London, 1965.

John of Cronstadt, *Ma Vie en Christ*, Bellefontaine, 1979.

Dunlop, John, *Staretz Amvrosy*, London, 1954.

Elchaninov, Alexander, *The Diary of a Russian Priest*, London, 1967.

The Way of the Pilgrim, R. M. French, tr., London, 1954.

Silouan, *Wisdom From Mount Athos*, Mowbrays, London, 1974.

Bloom, Anthony, *School of Prayer*, Darton, Longman, and Todd, London, 1970.

Clement, Olivier, *Le Visage intérieur*, Stock, Paris, 1978.

————, *Le Chant des larmes*, Desclée de Brouwer, Paris, 1982.

Evdokimov, Paul, *Les Ages de la vie spirituelle*, Desclée de Brouwer, Paris, 1964.

————, *Sacrement de l'Amour*, de l'Epi, Paris, 1962.

Evdokimov, Michel, *Pèlerins russes et vagabonds mystiques*, Cerf, Paris, 1987.

Archimandrite Spiridon, *Mes Missions en Sibérie*, Cerf, Paris, 1956.

Archimandrite Sophrony, *His Life is Mine*, Mowbrays, London, 1967.

Colophon

Written by Elisabeth Behr-Sigel

Translated by Fr. Steven Bigham

Published by Philip Tamoush
Oakwood Publications, Torrance, CA

Typeset in *ITC Bookman* with
Adobe Helvetica running heads by
George Bedrin, *Orthodox Information
Data Associates [O.ι.δ.α.],* Grand Isle, VT, &
Nicholas Turnbull, *Atelier Analogion,* Montréal, QC

Proofread by John Barns

Cover designed by George Bedrin, *O.ι.δ.α.*